**WITHDRAWN FROM
TSC LIBRARY**

FLA/HC107.F63 E542 1991

DeHaven-Smith, Lance.
  Environmental concern
Florida and the nation

**A FINE WILL BE CHARGED
FOR EACH OVERDUE BOOK**

*Environmental Concern
in Florida and the Nation*

Environmental Concern
in Florida
and the Nation

Lance deHaven-Smith

University of Florida Press / Gainesville

Copyright 1991 by the Board of Regents of the State of Florida
Printed in the U.S.A. on acid-free paper

The University of Florida Press is a member of University Presses of Florida, the scholarly publishing agency of the State University System of Florida. Books are selected for publication by faculty editorial committees at each of Florida's nine public universities: Florida A&M University (Tallahassee), Florida Atlantic University (Boca Raton), Florida International University (Miami), Florida State University (Tallahassee), University of Central Florida (Orlando), University of Florida (Gainesville), University of North Florida (Jacksonville), University of South Florida (Tampa), University of West Florida (Pensacola).

Orders for books published by all member presses should be addressed to University Presses of Florida, 15 NW 15th St., Gainesville, FL 32611.

Library of Congress Cataloging-in-Publication Data

DeHaven-Smith, Lance.
   Environmental concern in Florida and the nation / Lance deHaven-Smith.
      p. cm.
   Includes bibliographical references.
   ISBN 0–8130–1056–X (alk. paper)
   1. Environmental policy—Florida—Public opinion. 2. Public opinion—Florida. 3. Environmental policy—United States—Public opinion. 4. Public opinion—United States. 5. Environmental protection—Florida—Public opinion. 6. Environmental protection—United States—Public opinion. I. Title.
HC107.F63E542   1991   90–47677
363.7′009759—dc20   CIP

Contents

Preface   vii

1. Environmental Belief Systems   1
   National Opinion Data.   2
   Social Structure and Public Opinion.   3
   Local Reactions to Global Problems.   8
   A Framework for Analysis.   9

2. The Locus of Environmental Concern   15
   The Geography of Environmentalism.   15
   Sources of Environmental Localism.   20
   Flaws in the Standard Measure of Environmental Concern.   21

3. The Organization of Environmental Belief Systems   23
   The Florida Context.   23
   Public Opinion.   27
   The Roots of Environmentalism.   33

4. Conceptualization of Environmental Issues   36
   Development and Elite Discourse in the Treasure Coast Region.   37
   Conceptualization of Land Use Controls.   39
   The Environment as Everyday Experience.   47

5. The Perceptual Screen — 49
Sunrise. — 50
Lee County. — 55
Delray Beach. — 59
The Visibility Principle. — 63

6. Evaluating Options and Tradeoffs — 66
The Fiscal Calculus. — 68
The NIMBY Syndrome. — 73
Environmental Publics and Coalition Politics. — 80

7. Environmental Publics in Motion — 82
Regulating Paradise. — 82
A Loss of Environmental Will. — 86
The Inherent Instability of Environmental Opinion. — 91

8. Environmentalism at the Grass Roots — 93
The Formation of Environmental Opinion. — 94
Implications. — 96
The Future of Environmentalism. — 98

Appendix — 101
Notes — 115
References — 129

Preface

THIS BOOK APPLIES A widely accepted thesis in political science to an area of public opinion that generally has been the purview of psychologists and sociologists. The thesis from political science is simply that most people do not conceptualize political issues in very sophisticated terms. The area of opinion examined in the book is attitudes toward the environment and environmental policy.

Given the complexity of contemporary environmental problems, one might expect analysts to assume from the outset that the average citizen has little in-depth understanding of environmental issues. After all, since the late 1960s most of the alarms sounded about environmental degradation have been based on technical scientific theories about population dynamics, natural selection, the global ecosystem, and other very complicated processes. It is doubtful that the public has much real knowledge of these theories, much less of their implications for public policy.

And yet analysts in psychology and sociology have assumed almost without exception that environmental opinion among the mass public is akin to the views of scientists and other elites. Admittedly, they have not stated this premise explicitly, and most would probably disavow the assumption if asked about it outright. But the premise is implicit in the methodology they have used to study environmental attitudes and in the questions they have asked.

Generally their research strategy has been first to develop a measure of concern for some aspect of the environment and then to identify the measure's demographic and ideological correlates. In some cases, the measure has included attitudes toward a variety of environmental problems or policies (for example, see Dunlap, Gale, and Rutherford, 1973; Maloney and Ward, 1973; Buttel and Flinn, 1974; Weigel and Weigel, 1978). In other instances, the focus has been on "growth management concern" (Baldassare, 1984; Connerly, 1986), "nuclear power opinion" (Webber, 1982), "concern for pollution" (Cutter, 1981), or concern about some other specific environmental issue.

However, regardless of whether the measure is broad or narrow, this approach conceives of environmental concern as a single state of mind that people experience in varying degrees. In theory, some people are not at all worried about the environment, others are alarmed only modestly and only about a few factors, and still others are intensely concerned about a whole slew of things. Because the research methodology measures the amount or scope of each individual's concern on the same dimension, it is, in effect, a search for people who have a range of concerns that is as wide as that of scientists or sophisticated environmental leaders.

There are several reasons why this research strategy was adopted. Attitude scaling is common in psychology and sociology to identify personality types and the traits of social classes, so there was a methodological predisposition in the disciplines when they began to study environmental opinion. Also, the idea of an environmental "movement" is widespread, and hence it probably seemed appropriate to search for individuals who were motivated by an environmental ethos. Finally, of course, much research in social science is intended to replicate or extend the work of others, so once the approach had been used in a few studies, similar research followed and the methodology tended to take on a life of its own.

What the approach failed to consider is that environmental opinion even among interested publics actually may be very diverse, crude, fragmented, and narrow. If it is, people's environmental concerns will vary not by degree but by substance. One group will worry about one issue while a second group will be concerned about something entirely different. To observe these narrowly focused perspectives, a methodology is needed that allows for ideological incommensurability between respondents rather than one that lumps everyone together on a single ideological continuum.

The research presented in this book employed such an approach.

Public opinion surveys were conducted nationally and in different locales in Florida, using open-ended questions and various analytic techniques to expose and explore the perspectival nature of environmental belief systems.

All of the surveys were run between 1983 and 1989. The analysis includes a national survey; a statewide poll; a regionwide survey of four counties in southeast Florida; and separate surveys in various counties and cities with different demographic characteristics and unique land use problems. The surveys were all conducted by the Social Science Research Laboratory at Florida Atlantic University. Computer-assisted telephone interviewing was employed. Detailed descriptions of the sampling methodology and question wording are contained in the chapter notes.

All of the Florida surveys were conducted in areas experiencing rapid population growth and associated problems. County scores on a number of indicators are presented in the Appendix to provide the reader with an assessment of how the study sites compare to each other and to other locales around the state. Because they are rather general measures all of the indicators have weaknesses, and these are discussed in the Appendix. But they are the best quantitative data of this sort available for Florida's counties.

Several institutions have supported my research on public opinion. The Florida Atlantic University Foundation provided a grant to establish the FAU Social Science Research Laboratory. The Florida Atlantic University/Florida International University Joint Center for Environmental and Urban Problems contributed funding for several of the surveys, as did the Florida Institute of Government. The Florida Department of Community Affairs supported two surveys of the Florida Keys. Other surveys were paid for by the local governments of the jurisdictions in which they were conducted. They included the Treasure Coast Regional Planning Council; the Lee County Board of Commissioners; the Palm Beach County Board of Commissioners; the Delray Beach City Council; and the Sunrise City Council.

I owe special thanks to Mrs. Sandra Franklin for helping me prepare the manuscript for publication. Also appreciated is the assistance of Mr. Lawrence Kastancuk and Mrs. Teresa Herrero in designing and administering several of the surveys. Finally, I am grateful to the staff of the University of Florida Press and the University Presses of Florida for their support throughout the publication process.

1
Environmental Belief Systems

DESPITE ALMOST TWENTY years of research, analysts remain undecided about the scope, depth, and intensity of the public's environmental concerns. The environment became a topic of widespread alarm in the late 1960s. Gallup surveys found a huge increase between 1965 and 1970 in the percentage of Americans who identified air and water pollution among the three problems they most wanted government to address during the next two years. In 1965, pollution was identified by only 17 percent of the respondents. Just five years later the figure was 53 percent. Similarly, in 1970 environmental issues made their first appearance in Gallup's open-ended question regarding the nation's most serious problems. Without cues of any kind, 4 percent of a national sample cited the environment as the most serious problem facing the nation.

What remains a mystery is whether these and other expressions of environmental concern actually reflect strong feelings and sophisticated perspectives. Two conflicting views are prevalent, one from sociology and the other from political science.

The hypothesis from sociology is that the public has a fairly well-developed environmental philosophy that covers a range of specific issues. The very idea of an environmental movement presupposes that a sizable part of the population has been mobilized for collective action to achieve common goals. The public's environmental concerns are seen by many analysts as rooted in a new awareness that the planet's ecosystem is fragile and requires far-reaching protection.

In contrast, political scientists have been more likely to view environmentalism as a passing fancy, a fleeting apprehension of a fickle public. This position was expressed well by Anthony Downs in 1972 when the environmental movement was at its height in the United States. Downs claimed that environmental concern was the type of issue that passes quickly through the "issue attention cycle" of public opinion. Environmentalism would be short-lived, he predicted, because environmental problems affect a minority of the population and the problems are generated by social arrangements that provide benefits to powerful groups (Downs, 1972, p. 45).

National Opinion Data

National opinion data seem to cut both ways. On one hand, the data offer support for the claim that environmentalism is a passing issue. Although in the early 1970s Americans started expressing concerns about environmental problems, their concerns do not appear ever to have been very intense. At the height of the public's environmental concern in the 1970s, the environment was ranked as the nation's most serious problem by no more than 7 percent of the population (Gallup Opinion Index, No. 60, 76, 78, 100). Such other problems as inflation, political corruption, war, and crime have always been more important to the public than environmental protection.

Moreover, the public has been unwilling to make significant sacrifices for environmental controls. A number of polls conducted in the early 1970s found that while more and more people said they would pay higher taxes to reduce pollution, the amount they were willing to consider was quite small—usually in the neighborhood of $1 per month (Springer and Constantini, 1974, p. 201).

On the other hand, the view that environmentalism is indicative of deep changes in people's orientation to nature is supported by the stability of environmental opinion over the past decades. Between 1973 and 1981, the Roper Organization conducted eight surveys at regular intervals, asking whether "environmental laws and regulations have gone too far, or not far enough, or have struck about the right balance." In every year, the combined figures for the "not far enough" and "right balance" options never departed more than 3 percentage points from 66 percent (Anthony, 1982). Even in 1981, immediately after the electorate had supported Ronald Reagan for the presidency, 31 percent of the respondents said that environmental regulation had not gone far enough and 38 percent said that it had struck the right balance, for a combined figure of 69 percent. Thus in the 1980s, despite a widespread and growing dissatisfaction with the size of government and the bureaucratization of politics (see *U.S. News and World Report*, 13 February 1978), the public continued to support extensive regulation for environmental protection.

Social Structure and Public Opinion

Is the public's environmentalism a philosophical reaction to global environmental degradation or instead a shallow response to local problems? The thesis of this book is that it is both. Environmentalism clearly stems, however indirectly, from worldwide problems of resource depletion, pollution, and overpopulation, but the public sees these problems very crudely, through narrowly focused eyes. The two perspectives on environmentalism mentioned above are simply two sides of the same coin.

Environmentalism as a Social Movement

The thesis that the public's environmentalism reflects a new and enduring philosophy was developed in sociology because sociology deals with social change at the level of culture and social structure. At least three sociological theories bear on environmentalism: structural functionalism, conflict theory, and the "new social movements" theory. Each conceptualizes social movements differently and offers a particular way of looking at environmentalism, but all three agree in suggesting that the public's environmental concerns are deep and likely to persist.

A good example of structural functionalism is John Wilson's (1973) book, *Introduction to Social Movements*. According to Wilson, social movements follow a linear pattern of development. They arise due to the inability of existing institutions to meet widespread needs or demands, they produce change, and then they become part of the institutional order. When a social movement becomes institutionalized, it changes its identity and is transformed into either a pressure group or an interest group. It becomes a pressure group if its goals have been largely attained but must be protected and perhaps extended. It becomes an interest group if its objective was economic gain for a particular category of people.

When we look at the environmental movement through the theoretical lens provided by functionalism, we see organized pressure and a responsive institutional order. In theory, new technology caused the environment to be harmful to a significant number of people. These people organized with the goal of cleaning up the environment and preventing further problems. The movement attained its goal in the 1960s and 1970s when laws were enacted for environmental protection, and then the movement became institutionalized and turned into a pressure group.

Conflict theory provides a similar analysis of the *origins* of social movements, but it reaches much more pessimistic conclusions about the ability of social movements to produce meaningful change. An example of this theory is Roberta Ash's (1972) book, *Social Movements in America*. Like structural functionalism, conflict theory views social movements as conscious, organized reactions to problems in the institutional order, but, unlike functionalism, it argues that most social movements are coopted. Cooption occurs when persons involved in a social movement are placed in elite-sponsored positions. The social movement is then transformed into an institutionalized movement that is structurally and ideologically incorporated into existing social and political relations.

From this perspective, the environmental movement was transformed to fit within the prevailing institutional order. It began as a radical challenge to the capitalist system, rejecting consumption, unrestricted economic growth, and exploitation of the natural environment. However, the power structure accommodated and coopted the movement by making marginal adjustments to economic activity. The capitalist imperative of unlimited economic growth was maintained, even though many of the relatively innocuous demands of the environmental movement were met.

The third theory—the new social movements theory—was proposed by scholars from Europe. Examples of their viewpoint are available in a recent edition of *Social Research* (Winter 1986). What distinguishes their perspective from the functionalist and conflict theories is their thesis that the "new" social movements, particularly for environmental protection and nuclear disarmament, are part of an ongoing transformation in world culture. The functionalist and conflict theories imply that the environmental movement has been institutionalized and is no longer a radical force in politics. In contrast, the new social movements theory implies that the environmental movement is just beginning.

According to this theory, new social movements differ from earlier movements in that they seek to protect the interests of the world rather than simply the interests of a narrow social or economic group. The new social movements are concerned with the survival of humankind in general. From this perspective, environmentalism is indicative of a worldwide change in public opinion. People increasingly see their interests as common to those of a world community.

Public Opinion Theory
Public opinion theory from political science raises a significant challenge to the sociological literature on social movements. In large part, the social movements literature assumes that the mass public is capable of sophisticated reasoning about the political-economic system. Structural functionalism, conflict theory, and the new social movements theory all conceive of the environmental movement as a philosophical reorientation of public opinion that was generated by national and global environmental problems. However, the thesis that people can be mobilized for abstract objectives like environmental protection flies in the face of findings from research on mass belief systems.

The prevailing theory of public opinion was developed in its clearest form by Philip E. Converse in "The Nature of Belief Systems in Mass Publics." Using national opinion data from the 1950s, Converse assessed the extent to which members of the mass public conceptualize political issues and candidates in terms of the liberal-conservative dimension used by policy makers and other elites. He argued that yardsticks like the liberal-conservative continuum are important because they allow the mass public to follow the complex discourse of policy makers without having to gather detailed information on the legislative process. In Converse's words (1964, p. 214):

> Under certain appropriate circumstances, the single word "conservative" used to describe a piece of proposed legislation can convey a tremendous amount of more specific information about the bill—who probably proposed it and toward what end, who is likely to resist it, its chances of passage, its long-term social consequences, and, most important, how the actor himself should

expect to evaluate it if he were to expend further energy to look into its details.

Converse used three different approaches for measuring the public's reliance on the liberal-conservative yardstick. First, he categorized the respondents' answers to an open-ended question about why they intended to vote for or against a particular presidential candidate. In the first or highest "level of conceptualization"—which was referred to as the "ideological level"—were placed those respondents "who did indeed rely in some active way on relatively abstract and far-reaching conceptual dimensions as a yardstick against which political objects and their shifting policy significance over time were evaluated" (Converse, 1964, p. 215–16). At the next level were the "near ideologues": those respondents who mentioned an abstract dimension but did not appear to rely on it very extensively. Third came the respondents who evaluated candidates in terms of "group interests," such as how the candidates would affect the working man, blacks, or farmers. Finally, the last two categories were evaluations based on "the nature of the times" and those which included no issue content at all.

Using this measure, Converse concluded that the liberal-conservative continuum is seldom used by the mass public. Among voters, less than 4 percent were categorized as ideologues, and only 12 percent as near-ideologues. A plurality of voters (45 percent) evaluated candidates in terms of group interests. The remaining 39 percent of the electorate—a substantial number indeed—relied on the nature of the times (22 percent) or had no issue content at all (17 percent) in their conceptualizations.

Second, Converse examined the extent to which the public's positions on specific policy issues are structured in left-right terms. If voters are consistently liberal or conservative, he argued, then their attitudes on various issues should be correlated. Converse found, however, that such constraint across issues was virtually nonexistent in the mass public.

The third test Converse made of abstract and sophisticated thinking on the part of the public was to measure consistency of people's positions on specific issues over time. Here the hypothesis was that voters might have idiosyncratic patterns of belief, each meaningful to the individual in his own way. However, Converse found to the contrary that most voters changed positions on issues more or less randomly during a four-year period, even though they usually continued to vote for the same party.

Overall, the conclusion that Converse reached on the basis of his research was that mass belief systems have very little breadth or sophistication. Rather than being organized around abstract principles that yield consistent attitudes across a variety of related questions, mass belief systems contain a narrow range of idea-elements that are based on immediate experience and are tied together very weakly by the diffusion of attitudes from elites. Most people vote for a particular political party on the basis of their group interests, and they have very little concern about questions of public policy.

Consequently, the public itself is fragmented, even at the most sophisticated level of conceptualization, into many narrow "issue publics." "One man takes an interest in policies bearing on the Negro and is relatively indifferent to or ignorant about controversies in other areas. His neighbor may have few crystallized opinions on the race issue, but he may find the subject of foreign aid very important" (Converse, 1964, p. 246). Moreover, like the mass public generally, these narrow issue publics themselves are characterized by a sophisticated elite leadership at the top but a very inarticulate and ideologically crude set of followers. Hence, said Converse, "it is likely that an adequate mapping of a society (or, for that matter, the world) would provide a jumbled cluster of pyramids or a mountain range, with sharp delineation and differentiation in beliefs from elite apex to elite apex, but with the mass bases of the pyramids overlapping in such profusion that it would be impossible to decide where one pyramid ended and another began" (Converse, 1964, p. 256).

As is typical in political science, Converse's findings met with both emulators and critics. Research that offered support for his views included a survey indicating limited adherence among the mass public to the nation's most revered civil liberties (Prothro and Grigg, 1960); two studies showing marked differences between the philosophies of group leaders and their followers (Wolfinger et al., 1964; Stallings, 1973); and a slew of national surveys confirming that, among the mass public, preferences for political parties are much more enduring than positions on public policy. (For a review of these surveys, see Natchez, 1985.)

Criticism of Converse's thesis has come from two directions. One argument is that mass belief systems are organized around dimensions that Converse's theory and associated observation methods fail to capture (Key, 1966; RePass, 1971; Pomper, 1972). Although Converse attempted to test for the possibility that individuals may have "idiosyncratic belief systems," his measure of stability over time focused on issues that could easily fall outside the range of many people's interests. In-depth interviews have shown that voters have coherent world views, but that politics is not very central to them (Lane, 1962).

The second argument against Converse's conclusions is that his findings are time-bound. Several researchers found that liberal-conservative consistency across issues increased in the 1960s when controversial issues arose and elites became polarized (Field and Anderson, 1969; Bennett, 1973; Nie and Andersen, 1974). This seems to indicate that under certain conditions the mass public is capable of conceptualizing politics in more sophisticated terms than Converse gives them credit for.

Despite these challenges, Converse's conception of mass belief systems continues to dominate the field. The charge that mass belief systems are integrated and coherent even though largely apolitical can be incorporated into Converse's notion of issue publics (deHaven-Smith, 1985b). Presumably, mass belief systems connect only tangentially, if at all, to the world of politics. Although there may indeed be "idiosyncratic belief systems," they have little content relevant to the liberal-conservative debate among elites or even to the narrower issue orientations of group leaders. Similarly, Converse (1973) has presented an alternative interpretation that attributes the changes in belief system constraint observed in the 1960s to changes in political stimuli rather than to increases in the cognitive abilities of the mass public. During periods of controversy, the mass public is given relatively clear signals about how issues may affect their group interests, and hence even though most voters are no more ideological or abstract in their thinking than at other times, they are able to be more consistent in their responses to questions about various policies.

Local Reactions to Global Problems

The point of contact between the two perspectives we have been considering resides in the relationship between systemic problems and the conceptualization of such problems in mass belief systems. The literature on social movements has made what appear to be, from the viewpoint of public opinion theory, some incorrect assumptions about the relation between sociostructural problems and political action. This does not necessarily mean, however, that a sociological analysis of the environmental movement has nothing to offer. Clearly, the emergence of environmental concern in the late 1960s was rooted in large-scale problems associated with advanced industrial societies, and the public's environmental concerns are likely to endure until the private enterprise system is modified to respect the ecosystem's limits.

What public opinion theory offers to this sociostructural analysis is a conception of how environmental problems, the warnings of scientists, and debates in politics are registered in the mass public. Most people are preoccupied with their everyday lives—their work, homes, family, and friends. For them, a philosophical orientation to the environment is unlikely. It is not that people are unconcerned about water and air pollution, energy shortages, and the destruction of wildlife species, but rather that they relate to these problems in very narrow and very concrete terms. The public's environmentalism is probably made up of many narrow concerns, none of which is necessarily shared widely.

Detailed analyses provide support for this conception of the environmental movement. Efforts by psychologists and sociologists to find a generalized "concern for the environment" among the mass public have been largely unsuccessful. Although one study has documented a relatively high degree of consistency between attitudes toward different environmental problems and policies (Tognacci et al., 1972), several others have concluded that environmental attitudes are issue-specific (Simon, 1972; Lounsbury and Tornatzky, 1977; Van Liere and Dunlap, 1981; Webber, 1982; Connerly, 1986). In particular, attitudes toward overpopulation, growth management, pollution, and nuclear power appear to be, at most, only loosely related. Also, different substantive dimensions of environmental concern have different demographic and ideological correlates, which suggests that various subgroups of the population have different environmental worries (Horvat and Voelker, 1976). Only age, education, and political ideology have been found to be consistently related to environmental attitudes, and even for these variables the observed relationships have been weak (Van Liere and Dunlap, 1980). Thus, the public's environmental concerns appear to be based not in an abstract ideology or philosophy but rather in immediate experiences that are relatively concrete and close to home. The environmental movement is a combination of many groups, all concerned about the environment, but in different ways and for different reasons.

A Framework for Analysis

The most important question for research on environmental attitudes is how environmental issues register among the mass public. It is easy to say that the environmental movement is a coalition of distinct publics, each responding to a different aspect of the conflict between economic growth and ecological limits. Much more difficult is identifying the particular problems that generate concern, the conditions that lead people to see a connection between various problems, and the relationship between people's concerns and their positions on controversial public policies. How are environmental problems translated into social action?

Elite Discourse and Mass Beliefs

Environmental opinion probably is formed through a complex interaction between elite discourse and the narrowly focused, socially rooted belief systems of the mass public. Sociological theories of social movements have assumed incorrectly that there is a fairly direct and unproblematic connection between environmental problems and the attitudes of affected groups. Public opinion theory complicates and adds realism to the sociological perspective by suggesting that most people will respond to environmental problems with narrowly focused concerns based on the arguments of elites plus their own individual circumstances. From this perspective, mass opinion is elite opinion refracted, disassembled, and absorbed into the context of everyday life.

The belief systems perspective is essentially a communicative theory.[1] It begins from the premise that elites develop sophisticated ideologies or philosophies because they discuss issues at length and must negotiate finely tuned compromises. The theory presumes further that these elite belief systems do not penetrate very deeply into the mass public. *Ex hypothesi,* group leaders and other activists articulate sophisticated viewpoints, but their positions are understood only in bits and pieces by the citizenry.

This communication failure has less to do with the cognitive abilities of mass publics than with the day-to-day routines prevailing in modern society. The average person has neither the time nor the inclination to acquire the background information necessary to understand the elites' arguments with any depth or sophistication. The bulk of what elites talk about is, so to speak, over the electorate's head. The few things that most people understand are those germane to their current circumstances, circumstances that vary depending on their social location and other factors. In theory, mass belief systems tend to be narrowly focused and perspectival precisely because the social structure in modern societies is complex and compartmentalized.

Elite discourse is crucial in the formation of mass opinion precisely because mass belief systems lack sophisticated conceptions of public problems. If the mass public were actually composed of people with knowledgeable and well thought-out positions on the issues, then the arguments of scientists and politicians would be relatively unimportant. The views of elites might provide new information or place a new slant on existing facts, but they would just be absorbed into the belief systems of the mass public, belief systems that, because of their complexity and breadth, would be critical of new input and able to incorporate relevant parts of it without themselves being radically restructured. In other words, a theoretically informed public would be unimpressionable, somewhat skeptical, and ideologically stable.

As it stands, though, the mass public is comprised of numerous belief globules that are almost entirely dependent on elite discourse for their connections to larger issues and ideas. The things that irritate and concern people in their workaday lives are very mundane—working conditions, taxes, traffic, development around their neighborhoods, and so on. The sophisticated ideologies presented by elites are like conceptual nets cast over the fragmented public that subsume and pull together these very crude and diverse orientations. Terms like "environmental protection" draw in homeowners worried about a nearby landfill, commuters annoyed with the traffic from urbanization, residents who fear pollution of their drinking water, hunters who want land left open and wild, and, of course, people who are alarmed about acid rain, global warming, endangered species, and other problems of a more regional or global nature.

Because of the globularity of mass belief systems, how issues are framed at the elite level has a considerable influence on the shape of mass opinion. If elites become polarized, as they did, for example, in the presidential contests between Johnson and Goldwater and later between Nixon and McGovern, then, as opinion data show for that period, the mass quickly becomes polarized as well. Conversely, comparatively consensual eras, such as the 1950s and 1970s, are characterized by a quiescent mass public that votes not on the basis of issues but on the basis of party, personality, and recent economic conditions.

The same holds for opinion with respect to the environment. If environmental protection is presented as a responsibility to future generations, it will generate one kind of reaction. If it is depicted as a threat to economic growth, it will spark quite another. No doubt actual conditions will play a role in how different people assess the arguments, but the arguments themselves will exert an independent influence as well.

A Causal Chain

The premises discussed above form a framework for research. Figure 1-1 is a rough sketch of the causal chain that needs to be investigated and clarified. The figure identifies several factors that intervene between environmental problems and the public's environmental opinion. Let us consider each link of the chain in turn, beginning with the relationship between environmental problems and the public's environmental concerns.

At this point, the environmental problems that register in public opinion have not been fully delineated from problems that go more or less unnoticed. It might be that in the mass public, "seeing is believing." People seem to be much more concerned about water and air pollution than about rising sea levels, overpopulation, or the destruction of the Amazon rain forests. On the other hand, it may also be that less weight is given to forecasted problems as opposed to those that are already occurring, because people have a naïve faith in technological fixes. Also important will be the particular problems stressed by public officials and other opinion leaders. In any event, the criteria implicitly used by the mass public in selecting targets of environmental concern remain unclear. Obviously, there is a perceptual screen of some sort and the factors stressed by elites certainly influence it, but we do not know the principles on which it operates.

Similarly, the nature of the public's environmental concerns has itself not been determined. Environmental problems are perspectival. Air pollution, for example, could generate concern for any one of several reasons—its unpleasant odor, the way it blocks the sunlight, its harmful effects on health, its possible effects on climate and sea level, and/or its connection to acid rain. That many individuals are concerned about a particular phenomenon does not mean that the nature of their concerns is uniform. In short, even after we identify the ways in which people select environmental problems for consideration, we need to examine how they relate to or conceptualize the problems thus selected. What is it about a given environmental problem that actually concerns people?

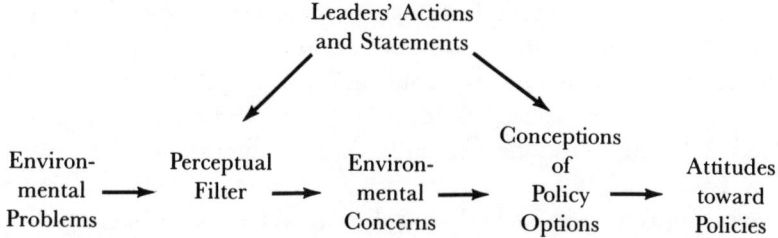

Figure 1.1. The Formation of Environmental Attitudes

Finally, the relationship between environmental concerns and positions on public policy must be studied. Air pollution may be considered by many people to be a threat to health, but antipollution laws will not necessarily be popular. There could be many intervening considerations—political values, beliefs about the costs of pollution controls, estimates of the effectiveness of such policies, considerations of fairness, and so on. Different considerations are probably brought to bear on different environmental concerns by different issue publics or categories of individuals. The arguments of elites are undoubtedly very important at this stage in the process of opinion formation, although in exactly what ways remains to be seen. We need to determine when environmental concerns lead to social action.

In the remainder of this book, these questions are addressed by a detailed analysis of public opinion nationally and in Florida. Florida receives special attention because its rapid population growth is causing a number of very different environmental problems that are being addressed at the local level in diverse ways. Florida has developed the nation's most complex and far-reaching system of state, regional, and local land use planning and regulation and the largest state program for public acquisition of environmentally important lands (DeGrove, 1984; deHaven-Smith, 1984d). Thus Florida provides a rich field in which to investigate the connections between environmental problems, elite discourse, and public opinion.

All but this and the last two chapters of the book focus on one or another of the relationships depicted in figure 1-1. Chapters 2 through 5 examine different aspects of the public's conceptualization of environmental problems, including how environmental concerns are organized in mass belief systems, the actual objects and experiences to which they refer, and the particular kinds of environmental problems that attract public interest. Chapter 6 investigates two aspects of the public's conception of its policy options: attitudes toward taxes and public services, and opinions about noxious public facilities such as landfills and airports. The not-in-my-back-yard or NIMBY syndrome is explored in detail. Chapter 7 is a longitudinal study of the Florida Keys that shows how issue publics form and reform in response to changes in the arguments and positions of elected officials and other leaders. The book concludes with a discussion of the theoretical, methodological, and practical implications of the findings.

2
The Locus of Environmental Concern

PERHAPS THE MOST BASIC question to ask about the public's environmental concerns is at exactly what geographical level they are directed. The theory of new social movements suggests that people are worried most about the global ecosystem, or at least about problems of national scope. What is supposed to make environmentalism new is that it is oriented toward the world as a whole rather than to the interests of a particular economic class or group. On the other hand, Converse's conception of mass belief systems implies that the average person's environmental worries are probably rather immediate and close to home, for Converse's thesis is that mass belief systems are organized around workaday experiences rather than abstract ideas. If the mass public's concerns extend to domains further out, it is only because the arguments and warnings of elites have tapped into their mundane peeves and pointed them toward a more distal referent.

In this chapter are presented results from a national telephone survey designed to determine the geographical locus of the public's environmental concerns. The survey was conducted in February and March 1989 and included 636 respondents selected randomly from throughout the continental United States.[1]

The Geography of Environmentalism

The survey's most important finding was that the environmentally concerned public is oriented mainly toward issues at the state and local

Table 2-1. Percentage of Survey Respondents Citing Particular Issues as the Most Important Problem at National, State, and Local Levels of Government

Issues	Levels of reference		
	National	State	Local
Foreign policy	7.1	0.0	0.0
Economic issues	9.1	18.9	15.9
Social issues	50.2	39.3	44.1
Government	20.5	11.2	4.9
Environment	6.0	18.8	16.5
Other	2.4	0.9	1.4
Don't know	4.7	10.9	17.2
Total	100.0	100.0	100.0
	N = 635	N = 635	N = 635

levels of government. Two approaches were used to gauge respondents' concerns at different governmental levels. One was a series of three open-ended questions that asked respondents to identify the most important problem facing "this country," "your state," and "your community."[2] Second, respondents were asked "how worried or concerned" they were about a variety of issues facing each of these political levels.

Environmentalism at Different Governmental Levels

Responses to the open-ended questions were classified into one of several categories (see table 2-1). Foreign policy included concerns about foreign affairs and defense. Economic issues encompassed concerns over the economy, jobs, agriculture, and economic development. Social issues included drugs, crime, the homeless, the poor, the elderly, education, housing, and moral deterioration. Government reflected respondents' worries over government issues or officials, taxes, and the budget deficit, while the environment covered both environmental protection and local growth and development issues. The "other" and "don't know" categories included miscellaneous responses and those who did not know or had no opinion.

The biggest disjuncture between respondents' concerns occurred as the context shifted from national politics. Foreign policy, social issues, and the performance of government were more likely to concern people when they thought about the national level of government than when they considered their state or community. Conversely, environmental protection along with economic issues were more likely to be cited as problems at the lower levels.

The jump in environmental concern as one moves closer geographically to the respondent is particularly striking. Although only 6 percent of the sample said that the environment is the biggest problem facing the nation, more than 16 percent said it is the biggest issue for their state or community.

The Range of Environmental Concerns

Of course, it is possible that the responses to the open-ended questions are misleading. Perhaps people have a broad range of environmental concerns at all governmental levels but the open-ended questions failed to elicit them because of the questions' emphasis on what respondents saw as the *most important* problems.

To test for this possibility, the environmental issue public was broken out and its attitudes on a variety of environmental issues at the three levels of government were compared to the attitudes of the remainder of the sample. Respondents were considered as belonging to the environmental public if, in answering the open-ended questions, they cited the environment as the biggest problem facing any of the governmental levels. The main difference between the two groups is at the state and local levels (table 2-2).[3] Although nonenvironmentalists show support for several forms of environmental protection, their concern for the environment does not extend (for a majority) beyond water and air pollution at the state level or to *any* issues at the community level. In contrast, a majority of environmentalists has several concerns at the lower governmental levels. At the state level, a majority of environmentalists is worried a great deal about water and air pollution, protecting agriculture, and protecting wildlife. Similarly, at the local level a majority is concerned about local water pollution and pollution of scenic areas, and large pluralities are worried about rapid growth and traffic congestion.

Environmental Concern in Select States

Still, it might be argued that environmental concerns are not necessarily focused on local conditions. Perhaps people worried about the environ-

Table 2-2. Percentage of Respondents Worried "A Great Deal" about Issues at the National, State, and Local Levels of Government

Issues	Environmentalists	Nonenvironmentalists
National		
Roads	29.0	30.1
Fuel shortages	35.2	34.2
Hazardous waste	79.3*	70.2*
Waterways	81.3*	71.8*
Toxic chemicals	71.0*	62.2*
Air pollution	65.8*	58.3*
Endangered wildlife	61.7*	49.9*
State		
Population growth	26.4*	14.6*
Types of people moving in	15.0	15.1
Roads	30.1	25.6
Preservation of scenic areas	62.2*	39.6*
Protecting agriculture	52.8	46.0
Water and air pollution	72.0*	59.0*
Protecting wildlife	55.7*	41.3*
Local		
Rapid growth	39.6*	13.0*
Types of people moving in	12.5	15.3
Traffic congestion	40.1*	23.2*
Quality of development	25.5*	14.7*
Pollution of scenic areas	53.1*	37.7*
Local water pollution	57.6*	47.5*
	N = 193	N = 439

*Difference between proportions significant in one-tailed tests at p<.05.

ment tend to focus on state and local levels of government because these levels are viewed as being closer to the source of the problem or better able to address environmental issues.

One way to get at this question as well as at the role of elite discourse is to examine public opinion in states with special environmental problems and aggressive state programs. DeGrove's (1984) study of environmental and growth management policies in the United States—the

Table 2-3. Percentage of Survey Respondents from California, Florida, South Carolina, New Jersey, Oregon, and Vermont Citing Particular Issues as Most Important Problem at National, State, and Local Levels of Government

Issues	Levels of reference		
	National	State	Local
Environment	6.0	28.9*	23.2*
Foreign policy	8.6	0.0	0.0
Economic issues	9.9	11.4*	8.6*
Social issues	51.0	45.6	49.0
Government	18.5	4.0*	2.7
Other	1.3	0.0	0.7
Don't know	4.7	10.1	15.8
	100.0	100.0	100.0
	(151)	(149)	(151)

*Significantly different from full sample in one-tailed tests at p<.05.

most comprehensive study of such policies yet conducted—lists the states cited in table 2-3 as having the most significant development controls in the nation.

Residents of these states definitely see the environment in proximate terms. Reference to the environment as a state or local problem is significantly more frequent in these than in other states, while reference to it as a national problem is exactly the same as in the rest of sample. In both the national sample and this subsample of states with environmental problems and growth controls, 6 percent of the respondents said that the environment is the biggest problem facing the nation. But 29 percent of the growth-problem sample said the environment is the most serious *state* problem, against only 19 percent for the national sample, and 23 percent said it was the most important *local* problem, as compared to 17 percent nationally.

These findings point to the interaction between elite discourse and the environmental localism of the mass public. Clearly there is a tendency for people to view the environment as a local rather than a national issue regardless of their area of residence. This is shown by the environment being cited by the national sample more frequently as a state and local problem than as a national problem. However, it is also evident that elite discourse affects mass opinion over and above this general predisposition to myopia. In states where top leaders have focused on environmental problems and actually have taken action to correct them, people are much more likely to see the environment as a state or local issue than are people in other, less environmentally progressive states. Thus leaders can take advantage of the public's localism by highlighting environmental issues that are comparatively proximate rather than distal. Presumably, the further away an environmental problem occurs, the more difficult it will be to mobilize widespread public concern.

Sources of Environmental Localism

It is difficult to sort out the relative importance of elite discourse on the one hand and the predisposition of mass belief systems on the other hand in generating the local orientation of environmental opinion because both factors have been and continue to be operative simultaneously. It is easy to understand why people naturally would think of environmental problems as local issues, for this is indeed the way environmental problems are experienced. While issues such as oil spills, global warming, and endangered species occasionally capture national attention, the problems that affect most people's real-life experience tend to occur locally and in isolation. The environmental issues that hit home are smog, water pollution, the loss of open space, and the destruction of special wildlife in one's own state or community. It should not be surprising, then, that when most people speak of "the environment" and of "environmental problems," or when they answer abstract questions about specific environmental issues, they have in mind conditions that are close by and that are likely to affect them personally in their daily lives.

At the same time, environmental policy has also turned from national issues to problems at the state and local levels of government, and this too has probably contributed to the public's environmental localism. When pollution and related problems emerged as issues in the early 1970s, there was a burst of legislative activity at the federal level aimed at protecting the integrity of the natural environment. Since then, however, most of the new initiatives in environmental policy have come from state governments and have focused on problems that are quite mundane—

urban sprawl, unsightly signs and billboards, local water shortages, and excessive development along beaches and rivers. Under intense pressure by aroused citizens, a number of states undergoing rapid population growth have developed policies to promote compact urban development and assure that public facilities do not become overloaded. Although their approaches vary, Hawaii, Oregon, Florida, New Jersey, Vermont, South Carolina, and California have all developed "growth management" policies of one sort or another (Bosselman and Callies, 1972; Healy, 1976; Pelham, 1979; DeGrove, 1984). The result, as we have seen, is that environmental issues, which already tend to be viewed as local concerns, are especially localized in these particular states.

Flaws in the Standard Measure of Environmental Concern

Although it is rather straightforward, the notion that the environment is conceived as a local rather than a national problem has far-reaching implications for survey research on environmental opinion. Perhaps most important, it means that the usual approach to studying public opinion toward the environment is flawed. Questions that refer to the national context tend to underestimate the frequency of environmental concern, since people are less likely to see the environment as a national problem than as a state or local one. Because of this measurement bias, for two decades analysts have probably underestimated the extent to which the public is alarmed about environmental degradation.

Certainly the well-publicized Gallup polls have been far off the mark. In the Gallup polls cited in table 2-4, the Gallup question unfortunately presents a geographical frame of reference that is quite distant from respondents' actual environmental concerns. If the question had referred to local government or to the respondents' communities rather than to "the country," the environment would have been cited much more frequently than it was.

This measurement weakness makes sense of the seemingly contradictory findings on environmental opinion discussed in the previous chapter. Analysts have been hard pressed to explain the observation that environmental concern as measured by questions about specific issues has been strong and stable even though it has been almost nonexistent in the open-ended questions asked by Gallup. In actuality, the Gallup results are misleading.

To understand the environmental movement, analysts should stop

Table 2-4. Percentage of Respondents Citing Particular Issues as Most Important Problem Facing the Country

Issues	1971	1975	1980	1984	1987
Environment	6	1	*	1	*
Foreign policy	22	4	15	22	21
Economic issues	11	84	70	39	22
Social issues	46	15	12	14	25
Government	4	14	12	19	21
Other	1	3	4	2	1
Don't know	4	3	4	3	4
	94	124**	117**	100%	94
	(1,568)	(1,553)	(1,593)	(1,518)	(1,571)

*Less than .5%.
**Adds to more than 100% due to multiple responses.
Source: Gallup: 1971, 1975, 1980, 1984, 1987.

asking questions about environmental problems in the abstract and should turn their attention instead to issues of state and local land use regulation. Ecologists and environmentalists may be aroused about the global ecosystem, but the vast majority of people is concerned mainly about the land, air, buildings, and landscape in their own states and communities.

3
The Organization of Environmental Belief Systems

THAT ENVIRONMENTAL CONCERNS HAVE proximate rather than distal referents says nothing about the organization or sophistication of environmental belief systems. Even though people are oriented mainly toward their own surroundings, they could have complex and well-informed views about environmental issues at the state and local levels of government. Of particular importance is determining the range of issues that environmental belief systems cover. Converse's theory implies that environmental perspectives will be very narrowly focused because they lack the conceptual sophistication to comprehend the connections between disparate conditions. However, it is possible that the immediacy and relevance of the state and local environment may foster more sophisticated belief structures than Converse found with respect to national politics.

A study of environmental issues in Florida is presented in this chapter. The aim of the research was to determine the range of environmental problems of concern to the Florida voter.

The Florida Context

Florida has one of the highest rates of population growth in the nation.[1] Between 1960 and 1980, the state's total population almost doubled, growing from a little less than 5 million at the start of the period to

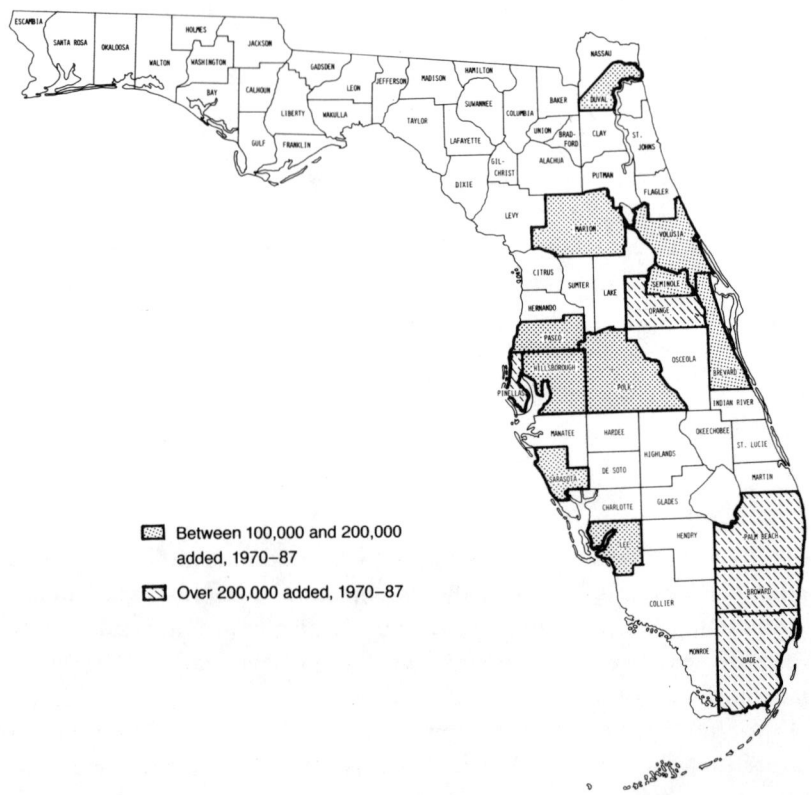

Figure 3.1. High-Growth Counties in Florida

almost 10 million at the end. For more than two decades now, an average of more than 200,000 people have been added to the population each year. That amounts to 540 persons every day—or twenty-two per hour, day and night. Expectations are that this growth will continue for at least the rest of this century. By the year 2000, Florida will have almost 15 million residents, three times what it had at the start of the 1960s.

Most of the increase in population has occurred along the southeastern and southwestern coasts and in an urban corridor running from Tampa through Orlando to Daytona Beach. Population figures by county for 1970, 1980, and 1987 are listed in table 1 of the Appendix.[2] Figure 3-1 is a map highlighting the high-growth counties. The geographical location of the state's population growth is problematic because the southern coasts and the state-center have much more complex and sensitive environments than the areas farther north.

Environmental Problems

The state's rapid population growth has caused serious environmental problems. (A thorough description of Florida's environmental problems can be found in DeGrove, 1984.) The most serious problem, considered against the state's desire for future development, has been the destruction of natural ecosystems, particularly with regard to the water supply. The southern region of the state is largely dependent for its water supply on underground aquifers, which are replenished by shallow surface waters flowing down the center of the state in the Everglades, a vast "river of grass."[3] As population growth has occurred in the coastal areas, and as fringe areas of the Everglades have been drained and developed, the water supply in the southern part of the state has been depleted. Government restrictions on water use are common during periodic droughts. Moreover, coastal communities experience saltwater intrusion into their wellfields as inland communities tap the water supply and reduce the underground flow of water toward the coast.

A related problem has been pollution of the underground water supply. Urbanization brings with it the use of hazardous materials. Dry cleaners and gas stations pose a threat to Florida's environment because their wastes can easily contaminate the state's underground water supplies. Similarly, the high-tech industry, which is generally but incorrectly viewed as a clean industry, also produces wastes that are dangerous to local wellfields. Unlike surface water pollution, which can be tracked to its source and prohibited, groundwater pollution moves slowly through the aquifer, only to show up at some distant point years later with no visible signs of its origins.

A third problem has been the destruction of wildlife species and habitats. Florida's state animal, the Florida panther, has been driven almost to extinction; it is estimated that only thirty panthers are alive today. Also threatened are eagles, manatees, and crocodiles. The panther and the manatee have received a good deal of public attention. Jimmy Buffet, a well-known singer from the Florida Keys, is featured on television commercials urging boaters to take precautions to protect manatees. The panther's plight is the topic of numerous newspaper articles and television news reports whenever another panther is killed (usually by an automobile on highways running through the panther's habitats).

Finally, Florida has seen a visible erosion in its quality of life. This is not to say that urbanization has had only undesirable effects; it has brought cultural diversity, increases in property values, and diverse forms of entertainment. But Florida's growth has also meant a fundamental change in the built environment. Because state and local governments have failed to keep public facilities abreast of growth, and because they have failed to regulate the nature, timing, and location of construction, many communities have overcrowded schools, unsightly mixtures of commercial and residential development, very limited public access to beaches and rivers, and never-ending traffic.[4]

Florida's System of Growth Management

In an effort to mitigate existing problems and avoid similar ones in the future, Florida's state legislature has gradually established a combination of environmental policies. (The following discussion is drawn from deHaven-Smith, 1984d.) Florida's system of growth management has three components: a framework of state, regional, and local land use planning; a process for regional review of developments of regional or statewide impact; and a program to designate and protect areas of the state in which unsuitable land development would endanger resources of regional or statewide significance.

Local planning is mandated under Florida's Local Government Comprehensive Planning and Land Development Regulation Act, which was passed initially in 1975 and then revised substantially a decade later. Through the development, adoption, and implementation of its local Comprehensive Plan, each local government is supposed to identify and manage the consequences of growth in its area. State direction is provided by state and regional review of local plans for compliance with Regional Plans and the State Comprehensive Plan.

Overall, the planning framework is designed to promote compact urban development and to assure that new development is served adequately by public services and facilities. Policies to encourage compact urban development include restrictions on development in wetlands and wildlife habitats, incentives to promote a greenbelt of agriculture around urban areas, and requirements for local governments to delineate urban and rural areas in their local plans and zoning ordinances. Along with these policies are requirements that public facilities be expanded commensurate with development. Regional Planning Councils and local governments must establish performance standards for all public facilities, and new development is prohibited unless facilities to serve the development are already in place or can be put in place as development proceeds.

The second component of Florida's growth management system, the Development of Regional Impact (DRI) review program, provides for the regional review, local approval, and state appeal of certain large-scale developments. Under state law, a Development of Regional Impact is any development that would have substantial effects upon the health, safety, or welfare of the citizens of more than one county.[5]

A developer proposing to build a project categorized as a DRI must submit an application for development approval to the local government with jurisdiction, to the appropriate Regional Planning Council, and to the Florida Department of Community Affairs. The Regional Planning Council prepares for the local government an advisory report on the development's regional impacts. The local government then holds a hearing and makes a decision to approve, approve with conditions, or deny the development.

The third component, the Area of Critical State Concern (ACSC) program, protects areas of the state in which unsuitable land development would endanger resources of statewide significance. Regional Planning Councils, local governments, and any other party may recommend suitable areas for designation to the Department of Community Affairs, which screens the proposal and, where appropriate, recommends areas for designation to the governor and cabinet. Once an area has been designated, affected local governments must prepare land development regulations that comply with the principles for guiding development set forth in the area designation rules, or else comply with state-adopted regulations.

Public Opinion

When considering public opinion on growth management issues in Florida, journalists and policy makers often make the same assumption that we encountered in reviewing the sociological literature on social movements. That is, they often assume that there is a direct connection between local environmental conditions and public opinion toward growth management policies. This premise is implicit in the view, common among political pundits of all sorts, that public opinion on growth management policies varies from one region of the state to the next, depending on local conditions. Support for environmental protection, water conservation, strict land use regulation, and similar policies is frequently thought to be concentrated in urban areas.

As we shall see, this thesis is not entirely inaccurate. There are indeed differences in public opinion as one moves around the state. However, the connection between environmental problems and public opinion in Florida is much more complex than most observers recognize.

The Distribution of Opinion

A statewide poll was conducted in the fall of 1984 to examine in detail regional variations in attitudes.[6] The sample was constructed so that three regions within the state—northern, central, and southern—had roughly the same number of respondents, thus allowing a comparison of attitudes across geographical areas.[7] The northern region, which is predominantly rural, is known locally as the Panhandle because it extends, in the shape of a handle, out from the Florida peninsula along the Gulf coast of Alabama. The central region is bounded in the north by Citrus, Marion, Alachua, Putnam, and St. Johns counties. It too is rural, except that it contains the rapidly growing cities of Tampa, Orlando, and the greater Daytona Beach area. The southern region includes Palm Beach, Broward, Dade, and Monroe counties. It is predominantly urban, but it contains the state's most sensitive ecosystems. Figure 3-2 is a map showing the three regions as delineated in the survey.

Two characteristics of the survey questions are noteworthy.[8] First, all of the questions were related to environmental policy reforms of one kind or another, thus assuring uniformity in the type of issue respondents were asked to assess with regard to different environmental problems. Second, all of the questions except one referred specifically to Florida policies or laws and hence provided the same referent to all respondents regardless of their geographical location in the state. The substantive issues included pollution, water conservation, wildlife protection, land use regulation, and economic growth that harms the natural environment.

Overall, the survey respondents were strongly supportive of the state's efforts to protect the environment and quality of life (table 3-1). A majority of respondents said that the natural environment is deteriorat-

Figure 3.2. Intrastate Regions

ing and that land use regulations should be strengthened. Respondents overwhelmingly supported stronger laws to prevent pollution and protect fish and wildlife from the hazards of construction, said that regulations for water conservation are needed, and opposed economic growth if it means the environment will suffer.

The only regional variation in attitudes on these growth management issues was of degree, not direction. Respondents in the central and southern regions were more likely than those in the northern region to believe that Florida's environment is getting worse, that land use regulation should be strengthened, and that water needs to be conserved. However, support for land use controls and environmental protection was also very strong in the northern region, certainly much stronger than prevailing analyses of the Florida public assume.

Table 3-1. Distribution of Opinion, by Region, on Selected Growth Management Issues*

	Northern (%)	Central (%)	Southern (%)	State (%)
Florida's environment is:				
Getting better	26	18	15	19
Getting worse	43	57	54	53
Not changing	28	21	27	25
Land use regulation should be:				
Relaxed	5	5	7	6
Strengthened	51	57	55	55
Left as is	31	23	23	24
Florida needs stronger laws to prevent pollution:				
Agree	84	82	88	84
Disagree	8	8	7	8
Florida needs stronger laws to protect fish and wildlife:				
Agree	87	91	89	90
Disagree	4	3	6	4
Water conservation is not needed in Florida:				
Agree	9	7	4	6
Disagree	78	82	88	83
We need economic growth even if it hurts the environment:				
Agree	11	12	11	11
Disagree	81	79	79	79

*"Don't knows" excluded.

The Organization of Opinion

The distribution of opinion discussed above does not tell us anything about how the belief systems of the respondents are organized. It could be that most residents have a broad environmental belief system and a wide range of environmental concerns, but it is also possible that any given resident has only one or two concerns and that the concerns vary from one individual to the next. In either case, opinion in the aggregate would appear the same, as a majority or plurality supporting policies to protect the environment in a variety of ways.

To examine the organization of opinion among individuals, a method was used similar to one of the approaches Converse employed in assessing the extent to which attitudes in the national public are organized around a left-right continuum. The sample was broken down by geographic region, and then, for respondents within each region, positions on different environmental issues were correlated.[9] The correlations indicate the extent to which individuals with a pro-environmental attitude on one question were similarly pro-environmental on other questions.

It should be noted that this approach is not without interpretive risks. Two factors need to be kept in mind. First, the measure of association used is Gamma. This measure is extremely sensitive to marginal distributions; it increases rapidly toward 1 or -1 as any cell in a two-by-two table approaches emptiness. Second, the frequency distributions for the survey questions lean heavily toward the pro-environmental response category and hence are likely to yield extreme marginals in the crosstabulations. All of this means that the Gamma correlations probably overdramatize some of the regional differences in the organization of opinion. On the other hand, the sensitivity of Gamma is useful in helping us to identify regional differences precisely because the correlation moves toward zero very rapidly as only a few people become inconsistent across issues.

All questions were coded to increase in magnitude with a pro-environmental stance. The hypothesis drawn from public opinion theory is that the particular issues on which respondents take consistently pro- or anti-environmental positions will vary as a function of geographical location because in theory people's environmental concerns are narrowly focused on their immediate situation.

The figures in table 3-2 indicate that public opinion in the northern and central regions is more fragmented than in the south. In the northern and central areas, two clusters of concern are evident. Opposition to economic development is associated with a belief that regulations are needed for water conservation, and support for stronger land use regulation is related to support for laws to protect wildlife and prevent

Table 3-2. Correlations (Gammas) between Environmental Attitudes for the Northern, Central, and Southern Regions

	Anti-economic development	Prevent pollution 2	Strengthen zoning	Prevent pollution 1	Protect wildlife
Northern					
Conserve water	.217*	−.277*	−.087	−.141	−.536*
Anti-economic development		−.190	.092	.121	.066
Prevent pollution 2			.365	.903*	.627*
Strengthen zoning				.206	.199
Prevent pollution 1					.468*
Protect wildlife					
Central					
Conserve water	.277*	−.176*	−.038	.103	−.609*
Anti-economic development		−.110	.053	−.001	−.254*
Prevent pollution 2			.216	.924*	.829*
Strengthen zoning				.042	.383
Prevent pollution 1					.769*
Protect wildlife					
Southern					
Conserve water	.453*	.285*	.074	.212*	−.158*
Anti-economic development		.368*	−.024	.358*	.352*
Prevent pollution 2			.577*	.915*	.764*
Strengthen zoning				.395	.686*
Prevent pollution 1					.766*
Protect wildlife					

*Chi square significant at .05 or better.

pollution. In effect, this suggests that environmental opinion in these regions is rooted in two separate issue publics, one opposing economic development because of limited resources (water) and the other advocating strong land use controls to prevent environmental degradation (pollution and the destruction of wildlife habitats). Moreover, the two publics appear to be in conflict, as indicated by the high negative correlation between positions on water conservation and wildlife protection. Crosstabulations (not shown) reveal that in the northern and central regions those who favored regulations for water conservation were much less likely than other respondents to support stronger laws for wildlife protection.

In contrast, residents in the southern region of the state where environmental problems are concentrated have relatively high, positive correlations between almost all of the questions under consideration. Although two correlations are negative, the negative correlations are quite low, and the overall pattern of correlations approaches consistency across issues. The average absolute value of the correlations is also higher in the south than in the northern and central regions. The average is .30 in the north, .32 in the central region, and .43 in the south.

The Roots of Environmentalism

As with environmental opinion nationally, the organization of environmental opinion in Florida probably flows from a combination of both local conditions and elite discourse. The role of local conditions in shaping the structure of environmental belief systems can be seen in the way that environmental concerns tend to mirror the configuration of environmental problems in the geographical area in question.

Casual observers of Florida public opinion have erred in assuming that attitudes toward individual environmental issues vary from region to region. Actually, it is not public opinion in the aggregate that varies but rather the way in which opinion is organized. Regardless of where one goes in the state, there is widespread support for environmental protection. However, in the northern and central regions of the state, where environmental problems have been relatively isolated and disconnected—water shortages occur in one area, pollution in a second locale, and loss of wildlife in the third—opinion is fragmented into distinct issue publics with narrowly focused and disjointed concerns. Support for one set of policies (water conservation and restrictions on economic development) is based in one group of people while support for another set of policies (land use regulation, pollution controls, and wildlife protection) is based in another. Conversely, in the southern part of the state, where a variety of regionwide environmental problems have been experienced simultaneously, the scope of many individuals' environmental attitudes includes a wider range of problems and policies, and residents are more united in their support for environmental protections of several kinds.

The influence of elite discourse in the organization of environmental opinion is visible in the conflict between the two issue publics in the northern and central regions of the state. At the risk of oversimplifying a great deal of diversity, most of Florida's organized environmental groups can be placed into one of two categories. One category is composed of traditional environmental protection groups such as the Audubon Society, Friends of the Everglades, and Florida Defenders of the Environment. Like one of the issue publics in the northern and central regions, these groups usually take a moderate position on growth management, supporting environmental protection but not opposing urbanization. In the other category are organizations like the Florida Wildlife Federation and the Florida Conservation Association, which are mainly concerned with recreational hunting and fishing. These groups tend to be opposed to population growth, often arguing that the state's limited water supply makes further growth problematic.

The finding from the statewide survey that the two issue publics in the northern and central parts of the state are in conflict is consistent with what is often observed at the leadership level among these two types of environmental groups. Frequently, the sportsmen groups are in disagreement with the traditional environmentalists. An example is the perennial debate over deer hunting in the Everglades. The sportsmen groups defend the hunting for its recreational benefits, while the traditional environmentalists oppose it on the grounds that unnatural declines in the deer population are in part responsible for the near-extinction of the Florida panther—deer are one of the panthers' main sources of food. Thus at the leadership level the environmental movement in Florida is divided over the issue of wildlife protection, a division that is also evident among the mass public in the northern and central regions of the state.

Extrapolating from Florida to the nation, this means that most people's environmental concerns are likely to be very limited unless the area where they live is experiencing a variety of difficulties or there is a clear consensus at the elite level on how to address a broad spectrum of environmental issues. If any given resident of North Florida is indifferent about all but just one or two of the problems occurring just a few hundred miles south, then it is fairly certain that mass belief systems generally do not encompass more than one or two environmental grievances. Because environmental worries vary from one individual to the next depending on local conditions, public opinion in the aggregate appears to be directed at a wide range of environmental problems, but the focus of any particular individual is actually remarkably narrow. Consequently, the influence of elite discourse on the organization of opinion is particularly pronounced. In effect, the debate among top leaders tells the mass public which concerns go together and which are in conflict. When elites disagree, the electorate sorts itself into opposing camps.

4

Conceptualization of Environmental Issues

ANOTHER ASPECT OF ENVIRONMENTAL belief systems still to be considered involves the conceptualization of environmental problems. It has been concluded thus far that the public's concerns have proximate referents and that the number of environmental worries experienced by any individual is probably rather small, especially if elite discourse is divided or fragmented. These findings clearly suggest that environmental belief systems are focused quite narrowly, but they do not foreclose the possibility that environmental opinion on particular issues is fairly sophisticated. One could imagine a number of publics, each having only one interest or peeve, but all possessing complex views and preferences on their special topics. On the other hand, it could also be that environmental belief systems are very crude.

Findings from a survey that attempted to determine how the public conceptualizes environmental problems and policies are examined in this chapter. The study was conducted in the Treasure Coast region of southeast Florida and probed people's reasons for supporting or opposing stronger land use regulation.

The survey question about land use regulation—discussed very briefly in the previous chapter—was employed in most of the surveys presented in this book. Respondents were asked simply whether land use regulation should be strengthened, relaxed, or left as it is. This question was selected to be a point of commonality between the various surveys because it offered a fairly specific referent to the responders—

controls over the nature, timing, and location of development—and yet it did not specify any particular objective. Stronger land use controls could be supported for any number of reasons: to protect the water supply, to keep office buildings out of residential areas, to require a certain style of architecture or signage, and so on. Thus the question was useful for splitting out the coalitions in support of, and in opposition to, Florida's growth management policies so that the attitudes of the two coalitions could then be investigated.

Development and Elite Discourse in the Treasure Coast Region

The Treasure Coast region is made up of four counties on the southeast coast (see figure 4-1). Running from south to north, they are Palm Beach, Martin, St. Lucie, and Indian River. During the past fifteen years, the population of each of the four counties has roughly doubled (see Appendix, table 1), but the pattern of development across the counties has varied widely. Only Palm Beach County, with a current population of more than 800,000, has much urbanization. Martin and St. Lucie counties have a number of large bedroom communities populated by retirees and by people who commute to Palm Beach County, and hence the development pattern in these counties is rural with some suburban clusters. Indian River County is largely rural throughout. The population density, and the increase in density between 1970 and 1987, are generally less as one moves north from Palm Beach County (see table 2, Appendix).

The policy debate over growth issues also varies across the counties. The leadership in Palm Beach County has emphasized capital facilities, particularly roads. In 1985, after leaders in the condominiums, which contain huge numbers of politically active retirees, complained about the traffic and demanded a building moratorium until roads were expanded, the county commission tripled both the gas tax and the road impact fee and passed an ordinance temporarily stopping development in areas where traffic congestion exceeded predetermined levels. All of these changes were fought by the development industry and hence were very visible. The impact fee was litigated and required voter approval in a countywide election before it could be applied within municipalities. Similarly, the ordinance that tied development approval to road capacity was the first of its kind in the state and took almost a year of public hearings to be worked out.

Figure 4.1. Treasure Coast Region

Whereas Palm Beach County has zeroed in on traffic, leaders in Martin County have attempted to prevent urbanization from spreading beyond Stuart, the county's main urban center. Martin County is home to several of Florida's leading environmentalists, including one who was an assistant secretary of the interior under Richard Nixon and is now president of 1,000 Friends of Florida, the state's most important environmental interest group. In the early 1980s, the county's environmentalists succeeded in persuading the county commission to establish an urban growth boundary around the outskirts of Stuart and to restrict development potential beyond the border. Since then, the conflict over growth has centered on whether new subdivisions and shopping centers should be approved when they are outside the designated urban growth area. In several instances involving large and politically influential development companies, the commission approved projects even though they were beyond the urban boundary and were opposed vehemently by local environmentalists.

The debate over growth issues in Saint Lucie and Indian River counties has been much less focused and systematic than in the counties to the south. Because at this point development has been scattered and isolated in a few large retirement-oriented subdivisions, disputes have revolved around individual projects rather than countywide issues such as traffic or the overall pattern of urbanization. As subdivisions or shopping areas have been proposed, they have been evaluated case by case, mainly with respect to their environmental and social impacts on the immediate areas in question. Objections raised in this context have included concerns about loss of agriculture, destruction of wildlife and wildlife habitats, and changes in the rural character of the community.

Conceptualization of Land Use Controls

The survey found that residents of the Treasure Coast region strongly supported controls on growth and development.[1] A majority (57.5 percent) of Treasure Coast residents said they wanted land use regulation strengthened, about one-third (35 percent) favored leaving land use controls as they are now, and only a very few (6.5 percent) advocated loosening things up.

An approach similar to the one used by Converse was employed to identify the ways in which Treasure Coast residents thought of Florida's environmental problems and policies. After the initial question on land use regulation, respondents were asked an open-ended question about why they took their particular position, either for strengthening, relaxing, or leaving land use regulation as it is.[2]

There was considerable variation in conceptualization. Table 4-1 crosstabulates positions on land use regulation by the reasons respondents gave for their positions.[3] The classification of rationales into "built environment," "natural environment," and "planning and zoning" was based on the particular object or domain of activity respondents discussed when explaining their positions. Representative examples of the kinds of responses included within each cell are listed in the table.

A plurality (46.5 percent) of those who wanted regulations strengthened cited problems in the planning and zoning process as their main

Table 4-1. Positions on Land Use Regulation by Rationale Given

	Strengthen regulations (%)	Leave as is (%)	Relax regulations (%)	Total sample (%)
Built environment	33.9	9.7	12.5	24.2
	Too many billboards, condos, office buldings	Regs make sure new houses are well built	Need more jobs, business in the area	
	Traffic is becoming worse, impossible	Keeps buildings, condos, at a low height, away from neighborhoods	Should be able to build what you want to	
	Road medians & new buildings aren't landscaped		Houses are starting to cost too much	
Natural environment	17.0	17.9	8.3	16.8
	The water is being polluted, used up	Must keep industry away from water supply	Animals are not as important as people	
	Eagles, panthers are being killed off	Need to keep access to beaches	It's hard to turn swamps into good land	
	The Everglades & farms are being spoiled, built on	It's enough to restore the Everglades		
Planning and zoning	46.5	9.0	25.0	32.2
	Developers always get their way	Planning ahead is important because of growth	Developers don't know what to expect, aren't being treated fairly	
	Can't tell if a big road or trash dump will be put nearby	Zoning must be flexible to allow change, progress	One neighborhood group can stop everything	
	No one is in charge; development just seems to happen			
No issue content	2.6	63.4	54.2	26.8
Total N	100 (230)	100 (134)	100 (24)	100 (388)

consideration. Among this group, references were frequently made to the effect that zoning decisions are arbitrary, that developers get preferential treatment, and that future development is unpredictable. This is a common theme in the local newspapers, but it does not show much understanding of the purpose of Florida's regulatory system. A second group (33.9 percent) who favored stronger land use controls did so out of a desire to improve the built environment. In addition to traffic, a central concern among this group was what might be called the uglification of the region. References were made to billboards, lack of landscaping, cluttered development, and the like. Another 17 percent of the respondents favoring tighter regulations said that environmental problems were the main factors influencing their opinion. The concerns of this group included water pollution and water shortages, the destruction of wildlife, and loss of agricultural lands.

Most of the respondents who wanted land use regulations relaxed or left as they are were unable to provide clear reasons for their positions. Those who wanted land use regulations left as they are tended either to say merely that existing regulations were "good enough," in which case they were classified as not having a substantive basis for their position, or they cited benefits from current policies—protection of the natural environment (17.9 percent), improvements to the quality of development (9.7 percent), or the assurance of adequate planning (9.0 percent). Those who favored relaxing land use regulation often said only that existing regulations were "too strict," in which case they were categorized as having no issue content in their positions. Other reasons given by this group included a desire for economic growth, lower housing costs, and broader property rights (12.5 percent), a perception that developers are being treated unfairly and that neighborhood groups are too powerful (25.0 percent), and a belief that existing regulations give too much weight to environmental concerns at the expense of ordinary people (8.3 percent).

Constraint across Specific Issues

On the face of it, responses to the open-ended question seem to indicate that people approach land use regulation from a variety of perspectives, most of which are very crude and unsophisticated. However, several objections to this interpretation could be raised. For starters, it might be argued that open-ended questions are indicators not so much of the conceptual foundations of people's belief systems but of their ability to articulate their views. Furthermore, the open-ended question used here had no follow-up probes, so it is possible that people with fairly sophisticated perspectives voiced only part of their concern when they responded. In short, perhaps people have much more abstract and complicated views about land use regulation than suggested by their responses to the open-ended question in the study.

To test for this possibility, respondents were asked a series of questions about very diverse issues surrounding Florida's system of planning and zoning. The topics included whether future development should be "compact and citylike" or instead "spread out"; the extent to which regulation should focus on environmental protection versus economic growth; the extent to which development should be conditioned on the capacity of the road system; and whether additional incentives should be given to farmers for keeping their land in agriculture.[4] The associations (Tau B's) between positions on these issues for the sample as a whole and for respondents broken down by the conceptual foundations of their belief systems are illustrated in table 4-2. The questions were coded so that high scores reflected support for the state's growth management strategies and low scores reflected opposition.[5] Thus relatively high positive associations between all of the issues would mean that the belief systems in question mirror the philosophy of the state's leaders, while low or negative associations would suggest that the belief systems have a narrow scope or at least depart from the state's growth management strategy.

Table 4-2 provides additional evidence that respondents conceptualized land use issues quite crudely. Note that the associations for the sample as a whole are much weaker than the associations where respondents with particular types of belief systems are treated separately. Presumably, the associations for the total sample are comparatively weak because the sample as a whole includes a variety of orientations toward land use issues. When all of these orientations are analyzed at once, the associations among items fail to reflect the amount of constraint between attitudes on certain issues that exists for individuals who share the same orientation.

The particular issues that are consistently related vary depending on the way in which respondents conceptualized land use regulation. Those who, in taking a position on the issue of land use regulation, voiced a concern about the built environment have an attitude cluster that appears to reflect a desire for high-quality, environmentally sen-

Table 4-2. Associations (Tau B's) between Issue Positions by Rationale on the Question of Land Use Regulation

	Density	Environmental risk	Infrastructure	Agland incentives
Total sample (N=328 to 383)				
Land use regulation	−.03	.09	.11*	−.02
Density		−.04	.01	−.03
Environmental risk			.23**	.02
Infrastructure				.06
Built environment (N=75 to 91)				
Land use regulation	−.05	.01	.04	−.13
Density		.19*	.15	−.05
Environmental risk			.25**	.02
Infrastructure				−.02
Natural environment (N=55 to 66)				
Land use regulation	−.01	−.05	.17	−.07
Density		−.18	−.13	−.01
Environmental risk			.36**	.32**
Infrastructure				.31**
Planning and zoning (N=112 to 124)				
Land use regulation	.00	−.02	−.09	−.12
Density		.08	.10	−.13
Environmental risk			.04	−.17*
Infrastructure				−.16*
No issue content (N=86 to 102)				
Land use regulation	−.13	.03	.00	.11
Density		−.08	−.01	−.06
Environmental risk			.13	.02
Infrastructure				.08

*Significant at .05 or better.
**Significant at .01 or better.

sitive urbanization. They consistently favor high-density development, strict environmental protection, and development moratoriums if roads become overloaded. Positions on land use regulation and incentives for keeping land in agriculture are outside the range of this group's belief system, which suggests that respondents in this category are supportive of urban growth so long as it is adequately served by public facilities and does not harm the natural environment. In contrast, those who conceptualized land use regulation in terms of its effects on the natural environment appear to desire a rural pattern of land use. Like the respondents who were concerned about the built environment, they support environmental protection and adequate public facilities, but they also tend to favor incentives for keeping land in agriculture and to oppose high-density, citylike development. The other two groups—those who focused on the planning and zoning process and those who had no issue content behind their positions on land use regulation—evidence little consistency in their attitudes across specific issues.

Constraint among the Proregulation Group Only

An objection that might be raised at this point is that the classification of belief systems into those focusing on the built environment, the natural environment, and so on may actually have lumped a number of different points of view together and thereby obscured the fact that some of the belief systems under analysis are fairly sophisticated. Of particular concern in this regard is how differently the supporters and opponents of land use regulation within the same conceptualization category appear to have been evaluating the land use issue. For example, among those who were classified as having the built environment as their central concern, the desire of proregulation respondents to avoid the built environment's uglification seems very different from the antiregulation respondents' objectives of keeping housing costs down and promoting economic development. If a wide range of perspectives is being grouped under each orientation to land use regulation, then the Tau B associations between responses on specific issues would be weak even if some of the belief systems in question had high levels of constraint.

One way to check for this possibility is to examine the proregulation group separately. Table 4-3 contains the Tau B matrices for the proregulation respondents only. The land use regulation issue is not included because only one response category on this issue is involved, and the respondents classified as having no issue content in their answer to

Table 4-3. Associations (Tau B's) between Issue Positions, Supporters of Stronger Regulation Only

	Environmental risk	Infrastructure	Agland incentives
All supporters of stronger land use regulation (N = 229 to 267)			
Density	−.001	.06	−.02
Environmental risk		.22**	.03
Infrastructure			−.04
Built environment (N = 63 to 71)			
Density	.20*	.11	−.08
Environmental risk		.25**	.03
Infrastructure			−.03
Natural environment (N = 34 to 39)			
Density	−.22	−.05	.02
Environmental risk		.35**	.30*
Infrastructure			.31*
Planning and zoning (N = 97 to 105)			
Density	.08	.18	−.10
Environmental risk		.08	−.17*
Infrastructure			−.21*

*Significant at .05 or better.
**Significant at .01 or better.

the open-ended question are omitted because of the small number of proregulation respondents in this category.

There are only minor differences between the association in tables 4-2 and 4-3. This means that it is probably safe to conclude that respondents' belief systems are indeed narrowly focused and unsophisticated.

Land Use, Leadership, and Conceptualization

Despite the findings discussed thus far, still a third objection might be raised against the conclusion that the respondents' belief systems are very crude. Although the findings support the thesis that most people's views about land use regulation do not cover the full range of issues addressed by Florida's system of growth management, this conclusion does not rule out the possibility that the belief systems are rooted in

Table 4-4. Conceptual Foundations by County

	Palm Beach (%)	Martin (%)	St. Lucie (%)	Indian River (%)
Built environment	39.5	20.2	18.9	13.3
Natural environment	9.2	13.1	23.6	30.0
Planning and zoning	25.2	46.4	30.1	26.7
No issue content	26.1	20.3	27.4	30.0
Total	100	100	100	100
N	(119)	(84)	(106)	(90)

*Chi square significant at better than .001.

sophisticated perspectives. Certainly, in light of the data examined up to this point, it is possible that people have sophisticated philosophical or ideological orientations to land use regulation even though their views are narrowly focused and appear quite crude.

This issue can be addressed by examining the relationship between public opinion and land use. Support for stronger land use regulation was widespread throughout the region. A plurality or majority of respondents in all four counties favored strengthening land use regulation. The percentage ranged from a low of 47 in Indian River County to a high of 63 in Martin County. Less than 7 percent of the respondents in any of the counties said that regulation should be relaxed. The question, though, is whether people's views about land use regulation are based on abstract principles about urbanization, environmental protection, and the like, or whether they instead derive from concerns that are very concrete and close to home.

Table 4-4 crosstabulates the conceptual foundations of respondents' belief systems by their county of residence. The figures suggest that respondents' conceptualization of land use regulation depends on local conditions and the issues stressed by elites rather than on concerns that are general, abstract, and independent of local politics. An orientation toward the built environment becomes less frequent and a focus on the natural environment becomes more frequent as one moves north from urban Palm Beach County through suburban Martin and St. Lucie counties to rural Indian River County. The influence of both land use and leadership is evident. The built environment is of more concern in the urban than the rural counties, and especially in Palm Beach County, where top leaders have targeted road congestion as the most important growth problem. Similarly, the planning and zoning process is the main issue in Martin County, where debate at the elite level has centered on whether to approve development outside an urban growth boundary. The natural environment is stressed in the most rural counties, which also happen to be the counties where development tends to be assessed in terms of its direct effects on environmental conditions in the immediate geographical area.

The Environment as Everyday Experience

We now have a clear idea of how Florida residents conceptualize the state's environmental problems and specifically what motivates them to support the state's growth management policies. The first lesson to be drawn from the Treasure Coast survey is that sophisticated environmental philosophies that include concerns about a number of environmental problems are quite rare. Findings from the statewide survey, particularly in the central and northern areas of the state, gave us reasons to hypothesize that this was probably the case; the regional survey confirms this suspicion in detail. Support for stronger land use regulation is rooted in a coalition of groups with narrowly focused concerns.

From this conclusion flows a second and related point. The reasons why people support stronger land use controls often have to do with very mundane things. One of the most common complaints is the ugliness of the built environment. For many people, especially those in urban areas, land use regulation is a policy directed not so much at the natural environment as at the aesthetic qualities of cities and neighborhoods. Those concerned about environmental protection in the traditional sense of the term comprise only a very small component of Florida's growth management coalition.

Third, those who want land use regulations to be relaxed do not appear to be thinking of land use controls in terms of how they affect either the built or the natural environment. Given what we have seen so far, we can only speculate about the motivations behind their hostility to land use controls. Perhaps these people are politically conservative and oppose regulation of any sort, or maybe they are just cynical about state or local government. Whatever the case, their opposition to land use controls seldom appears to be connected directly to land use issues.

A fourth and final lesson is that environmental concerns are very sensitive to elite discourse at the local level of government. People throughout Florida are concerned about population growth and they support land use controls, but how they conceptualize growth issues is contingent on what top leaders say about development in their own areas. Depending on the concerns and arguments of local officials and environmentalists, growth in one area will conjure fears of traffic while in another it will spark alarm about the destruction of wildlife or cynicism about the politics of planning and zoning.

5
The Perceptual Screen

THE CONCLUSION THAT MOST people conceptualize environmental problems in very concrete and immediate terms says nothing about how they select environmental problems for consideration or the conditions that push them from indifference to concern. We can be fairly certain that the factors that trigger people to support environmental policies are quite mundane—water shortages, the loss of open space, smog, and other localized annoyances. But this does not tell us why some problems cause alarm while others are ignored.

In this chapter, public opinion is examined in three very different Florida communities: (1) the city of Sunrise, a rapidly growing but rather tranquil and homogeneous suburb near Fort Lauderdale; (2) Lee County, a predominantly rural county on the Gulf that is experiencing urbanization and suburbanization along its coastline; and (3) Delray Beach, a retirement community on the southeast coast that is experiencing a great deal of commercial development and an influx of younger residents. Our objective in examining these communities is to identify the effects on public opinion of different environmental and political contexts, so that we can get an indication of how the public's "perceptual screen" operates on environmental problems. All three communities are growing rapidly, but the type of development they are experiencing varies, as does the reaction to it by local opinion leaders and political officials. As we shall see, certain kinds of changes in land use and associated responses by elites cause strong public reactions while other changes and policies go more or less unnoticed.

Sunrise

The city of Sunrise is an upper-middle-class suburb in western Broward County. During the past fifteen years, its population has grown rapidly, from 7,403 residents in 1970 to more than 47,000 in 1984 (1985 *Florida Statistical Abstract*, table 1.69, p. 30). Despite this growth, Sunrise has experienced few, if any, land use controversies. Development has been predominantly residential along with some "strip commercial" shopping plazas and office complexes, and city officials have kept public facilities abreast of the expanding population. In short, Sunrise is rather idyllic, particularly when contrasted with many of the communities nearby.

The only political event of note was a rather lengthy scandal involving the city's longtime mayor. During the 1970s, the mayor was indicted several times for using his office for financial gain. In each case he was exonerated, but in 1985 he was convicted of criminal charges and has since served time in a Florida prison.

A public opinion survey was conducted in Sunrise during July 1986.[1] Financed by the city council, it was undertaken because of a desire by city officials to be responsive to the citizenry following the scandal involving the mayor. Thus, unlike the other surveys discussed in this chapter, this one was not initiated because of intense public controversy over changing patterns of land use.

Public opinion in Sunrise can be summarized in a few words: Residents are highly satisfied with the city. Land use regulation, environmental protection, and related issues are neither controversial nor salient.

Perceptions of Problems

Support for this sanguine conclusion about public opinion in Sunrise was found in several areas. First, most respondents in the public opinion survey did not think the city had any major problems. Respondents were asked a series of questions about whether they would rate three issues as "big problems": road conditions, crime, and traffic (table 5-1).[2]

The responses to this set of questions are quite remarkable. Most

Table 5-1. Percentage of Sunrise Respondents Who Said that the Following Issues Are Big Problems

	%	N
Condition of the roads	23.8	103
Traffic	50.2	217
Crime	31.2	135

respondents (73.3 percent and 63.4 percent, respectively) did not view either the conditions of the roads or crime as a problem in their city. The remaining issue, traffic, was viewed as a problem by only a slim majority (50.2 percent) of the residents. This distribution of opinion is remarkable because statewide surveys and surveys conducted in other parts of southeast Florida have found high levels of citizen concern about these issues, particularly crime and traffic. For example, a 1985 statewide survey conducted by the *Miami Herald* found crime rated as a "big problem" by two-thirds of Florida's adult residents. In southeast Florida, where Sunrise is located, an even larger majority cited crime as a major issue. (See the *Herald's* edition on 17 February 1985, pp. 1–2D.) Similarly, the survey of the Treasure Coast discussed in the previous chapter found that 71 percent of the region's residents believe that traffic is a big problem.

The finding in Sunrise that traffic, road conditions, and crime are not seen as "big problems" held across most of the demographic variables included in the study. Crosstabs (not shown) revealed only a few exceptions. Of those living in Sunrise for more than twenty years, a majority (57.1 percent) perceived the conditions of the roads to be problematic, as did 53.8 percent of those residents earning more than $90,000 annually. The same relationship existed concerning the perception of crime as a problem, with 71.4 percent of those citizens having resided in Sunrise for more than twenty years, and 69.2 percent of those earning more than $90,000 annually, seeing it as a problem. Of those respondents viewing traffic as a problem, two groups stood out as having large majorities: residents living in condominiums and those 65 years old and older.

Certainly it is possible that residents had concerns about the city that simply were not tapped with our questions about road conditions, crime, and traffic. To test for this possibility, respondents were asked

Table 5-2. Open-Ended Question on Problems Facing Sunrise

What is the biggest problem now?	%	N
Social system	28.6	65
Services	26.4	60
Government	22.9	52
Built environment	22.0	50
Total	99.9	227

two additional questions after the questions on whether certain issues are (or are not) "big problems": What in their view was the biggest problem facing the city, and what did they think would be the biggest problem five years from now?[3] These were open-ended questions; interviewers simply wrote down whatever answers were given. Once the survey was completed, all of the responses to these questions were examined to identify some common themes.

The responses to the question about current problems are listed in table 5-2. Note that the total number of respondents included in this table is only 227 out of the total sample of 468. The low number in table 5-2 is due to the fact that many respondents either had no serious problems with the city or else their responses were idiosyncratic. Responses that were idiosyncratic in the sense that they did not fall into any of the observed patterns, as well as responses indicating that the city has no serious problems, were excluded from the tabulations. Examples of idiosyncratic responses included "needing a permit for everything"; having to travel to restaurants and shopping; problems with cable television; "having to pay for what the ex-mayor stole"; the arms race; and a variety of other concerns that were voiced by only one or two people. Thus, when examining table 5-2, it must be remembered that a large number of respondents are excluded and that this itself supports the thesis that many residents have no major complaints.

When the coders looked for common themes in the answers to the two open-ended questions, four major categories of responses were found. Twenty-eight percent cited problems with the social system. Examples included crime (drugs, robbery, and gambling); too many people; too many retirees; not enough young people; too many tourists; racial tensions; and conflicts between long-term residents and those who had recently moved to the city.

The next most frequently mentioned problem (26.4 percent) was public services. About half the people mentioning services were concerned with transportation problems, particularly traffic, speeding, bad drivers, and poor road conditions. The other half referred to poor schools, inadequate care for the elderly, and not enough fire and police protection.

Another 22.9 percent said that the biggest problem currently facing Sunrise had to do with the city government. Political infighting, inept public officials, and the city government's "poor image" were mentioned frequently.

Finally, 22 percent were concerned about the built environment. Responses in this category included concern about overdevelopment, poor zoning and zoning enforcement, and deteriorating neighborhoods.

With one exception, there was little difference between what people said is the worst problem now and what they expected to be the worst problem in the future. The exception was that very few respondents expected the Sunrise city government to be a problem in the future. Instead, respondents often said that in the future there will be more social problems. Apparently, and with some justification, residents thought that the city government was improving.

Public Facilities and Services

The second piece of evidence indicating that Sunrise residents are very satisfied with the city had to do with respondents' ratings of public facilities and services. The survey included both general and specific questions in this area.

At a general level, respondents were asked whether city services and taxes should be increased, decreased, or left as they are.[4] A large majority (69.4 percent) felt that services and taxes should be left at existing levels. Fifteen percent said that taxes and services should be reduced, while 7.6 percent favored increasing services and taxes.

The question on specific city facilities and services centered on the city's possible need for a more extensive bus system, greater numbers of recreational facilities and parks, and increases in police, emergency medical, and social services.[5] The percentage of respondents favoring increases in these areas is recorded in table 5-3. An increase was favored

Table 5-3. Preferences for Specific Services and Facilities

	Percent favoring increases	N
City bus system	29.5	132
City sports facilities	40.2	179
Number of city parks	52.0	232
City police services	35.5	158
City emergency medical services	26.9	120
Social services	43.6	194

by a majority of respondents for only one facility: 52 percent of the residents said that they wanted more city parks. For several services and facilities, the public was more or less evenly divided between increases and leaving them as they are now. This was true for the city bus system, social services, and city sports facilities. A majority of respondents said that emergency medical services and police protection should be left at current levels.

Positions on Land Use Regulation

The third area where Sunrise residents again expressed their satisfaction with the city was on the question on whether land use regulation should be strengthened, relaxed, or left as it is. Public opinion about problems and trends in the city is not necessarily related to preferences about land use planning and zoning. Those who believe that the city has problems could attribute them to a number of factors having nothing to do with construction and development, or they might attribute problems to development but not see land use controls as the solution. Conversely, residents who think that the quality of life in Sunrise is quite good might attribute it to effective land use controls and favor strengthening such controls in the future.

A plurality (47.4 percent) of the respondents favored leaving the city's land use controls as they are now. Slightly less than 35 percent said that land use regulations should be strengthened, and 10.7 percent thought controls should be relaxed. This distribution of opinion is particularly striking when it is compared to results from other surveys. Of all the Florida surveys discussed in this book—statewide, Lee County, the Florida Keys, the Treasure Coast region, and the communities along Florida's east coast—the percentage of residents who support the status quo is highest in Sunrise. Statewide, as we have seen, 55 percent of the public favored stronger regulation, 6 percent advocated relaxation, and only 24 percent wanted controls left as they are. Again, as with the questions about public services and facilities and about whether certain issues are "big problems," Sunrise residents appear to be remarkably satisfied with existing conditions.

Crosstabulations showed that satisfaction with the existing system of land use controls was widespread. However, a few groups stood out as wanting regulations strengthened: those who had lived in Sunrise for at least twenty years; respondents with graduate degrees; and those who were between forty-five and fifty-four years old.

Lee County

The survey of Lee County residents was conducted in 1984 when the county commission was in the process of reviewing and amending its local Comprehensive Plan. The county's population has grown rapidly during the past three decades, from about 21,000 in 1950 to more than 205,000 in 1980. This growth is expected to continue. By the year 2005, fewer than twenty years away, the population is projected to reach 429,000, more than double its existing level.

Until recently, most of this growth had been concentrated in and around the city of Ft. Myers, which is on the Gulf coast. Directly to the north and inland to the east of the city are two large subdivisions that were platted in the 1950s and marketed nationally as retirement communities but never were extensively developed because of inadequate public facilities. The remainder of the county is predominantly rural—either forestland, wetland, or farmland.

In revising its Comprehensive Plan in 1984, the county commission proposed to establish what was in effect an urban growth boundary. The large subdivision to the east of Ft. Myers (Lehigh Acres) was placed outside the proposed urban services area, as was a nearby parcel of five thousand acres whose owners were seeking approval for development as a Development of Regional Impact (DRI). However, under intense pressure during the planning process, the commission's efforts to channel future development into Ft. Myers collapsed. Both Lehigh Acres and the contiguous DRI were placed within the county's urban services boundary, and the stage was set for suburban development in a number of areas around the county.

Controversy over the local plan reflected the conflicting views and interests of the county's top leaders, but the final compromise was indicative of the relative strength of the progrowth and antigrowth forces at the grass roots. Lee County has some very active environmentalists. Porter Goss, then a county commissioner and now a U.S. congressman, gained fame in the 1970s when he fought successfully for strong land use controls on Sanibel Island, which is off the Lee County coast (see Babcock and Siemon, 1985, pp. 95–118). Goss was the most visible advocate for the urban growth boundary. On the other hand, two of Florida's largest development corporations (Coral Ridge Properties and Lehigh Development Corporation) opposed the urban boundary and tried to convince the citizenry that it was unfair to landowners and would harm the county's economic future. As we shall see, both the environmentalists and the developers were successful in mobilizing a certain amount of support for their positions. Consequently, the 1984 Plan ended up splitting the difference between these forces by keeping the urban services boundary but expanding its borders to allow large-scale residential development outside the city of Ft. Myers.

Land Use Regulation

The polarization of the citizenry was clear from the responses to our standard question on land use regulation.[6] At the time of the survey, 47 percent of the respondents in the survey said land use regulations should be strengthened, 24 percent wanted regulations left as they are, and 19 percent said that regulations should be relaxed. The percentage of respondents favoring a relaxation of land use controls was higher in Lee County than in any of the other communities discussed in this book, while the percentage favoring stronger regulation was near the state norm. Clearly, the Lee County public was divided over this issue. Support for stronger land use regulations was most frequent in the more rural, southern part of the county and, as usual, among the middle income groups.

The division of public opinion on the issue of land use regulation appears to have been based in the two conflicting concerns raised by the county's elites: fears about environmental problems, and preferences for economic development.

Table 5-4. Regulatory Positions by Environmental Perceptions

	Better (%)	No change (%)	Worse (%)
Relax regulations	27	20	15
Leave regulations unchanged	32	36	11
Strengthen regulations	33	31	64
Not sure	8	13	10
Total	100	100	100
N	(65)	(111)	(151)

Perceptions of Environmental Trends

The natural environment of Lee County is sensitive and complex. The county contains marshes, beaches, interior wetlands, and such rare wildlife species as the bald eagle and the Florida panther. In part, Lee County's natural beauty is what attracts people to the area.

At the time of the survey, the Lee County public was divided over whether the county's natural environment was deteriorating.[7] Forty-four percent of the respondents said that the quality of the environment in the county was getting worse. Thirty-three percent believed that it was not changing. Almost one-fifth (19 percent) thought that the quality of the natural environment in Lee County was improving.

Perceptions of environmental trends varied systematically with social and geographic location. Two variables—education and length of residency in the county—had fairly strong linear relationships with views of environmental trends. The longer respondents had been living in Lee County and the more education they had, the more frequently they said that the environment of the county was deteriorating. Length of residency had a breaking point; only about one-fourth of the respondents who had lived in the county less than three years felt that the environment was worsening, whereas about two-fifths to one-half of the other respondents held this view. Several other demographic characteristics also influenced perceptions. Males more than females, owners more than renters, people living outside Ft. Myers more than Ft. Myers residents, and people living in the southeastern and southwestern parts of the county more than those in the north, said that the natural environment of the county was getting worse.

Positions on land use regulation were influenced by perceptions of environmental trends. Figures in table 5-4 show that support for stronger regulation was greatest among respondents who thought that Lee County's environment was getting worse; almost two-thirds of those who said that the environment was deteriorating thought that land use regulations should be strengthened. In contrast, respondents with other perceptions of environmental trends were more or less evenly divided over whether to strengthen, relax, or leave land use controls as they are.

Economic Development

The economy of Lee County is centered around tourism, construction, and retirement. The average income in the county of $11,545 per year is about $1,000 below the state average (Lee County Comprehensive Plan, 1984).

A large majority of respondents in the sample favored a policy of active economic development. Respondents were asked whether the Lee County government should try to attract business and industry into the area or instead let the economy develop on its own.[8] More than two-thirds (68 percent) favored trying to attract industry, while only 22 percent opposed it.

Respondents also indicated that their preferences for economic development were fairly intense. Those who said that the Lee County government should try to attract business and industry into the area were asked how much more in taxes they would be willing to pay each year in order to have such an effort undertaken. The options, which were read as part of the question, ranged from none to two hundred dollars in fifty-dollar increments. Almost a third of the respondents said they would pay nothing, more than a third said they would pay no more than fifty dollars, and about a quarter said they would pay more than fifty dollars.

As would be expected, those who favored economic development were more likely than other groups to say that land use regulation should be relaxed. They were also less likely to think that the natural environment was deteriorating.

The Eye of the Storm

Responses to another set of questions revealed that the conflict between the environmental protection group and the economic development group centered around the county government, which of course is exactly where the debate between the county's top leaders was taking place. The public's perception of the locus of the issue could have been otherwise, for a number of governmental entities regulate land use in the area. The U.S. Army Corps of Engineers limits or prohibits construction in certain parts of the county, such as mangrove estuaries. The Florida Department of Community Affairs oversees implementation of the planning process. The governments of Lee County and the city of Ft. Myers zone land and either issue or withhold development orders.

To see if residents distinguished among various units of government, the survey asked respondents to evaluate land use regulation in the county by the federal government, the state government, Lee County, and the city of Ft. Myers. Specifically, respondents were asked whether each unit of government was regulating construction and development too much, too little, or about the right amount.[9]

Most respondents did not believe that any of the units of government in question was regulating development too much. The percentage of respondents choosing the "too much" category ranged between 7 and 18 across all four questions. Significantly, Lee County was the unit of government with the highest percentage of respondents saying that it regulated development both too much (18 percent) and too little (44 percent).

The thesis that conflict over land use centered around the county government was also supported when respondents' positions on the general question of regulation were crosstabulated with their specific evaluations of regulation by the federal government, state government, city of Ft. Myers, and Lee County. Among those who wanted regulation strengthened, the one unit of government that stood out as regulating development too little was the county government. At the same time, among those who wanted regulations relaxed, the Lee County government stood out as regulating development too much.

Delray Beach

During the 1960s, Delray Beach was a sleepy little retirement community. The city is situated in Palm Beach County on the east coast in the middle of an urban corridor running from Boca Raton in the south to West Palm Beach in the north. The population of Delray Beach and the surrounding area has grown incredibly rapidly during the past decade. Between 1970 and 1983, the population of the corridor increased by more than 80 percent, and the population of the city almost doubled. Delray Beach now has a population of about forty-two thousand.

As a result of this growth, the character of Delray Beach has been changing. What not long ago was a small coastal community with a village atmosphere is becoming a center of commercial development. Increasingly, the city is marked by contrast. Office buildings and hotels are located near residential areas; retirees, once the dominant segment of the population, are being joined by young professionals; the very poor are concentrated in neighborhoods not far from the well-off.

As in Lee County, the Delray Beach survey was conducted to provide information to elected officials while they were revising the local government Comprehensive Plan.[10] Prior to the Delray Beach election in 1984, several citizens' groups had organized in opposition to some large-scale commercial development the city council was planning to approve. In an effort to placate the citizenry, the city council appointed a Citizens Advisory Committee to review the local Comprehensive Plan and recommend changes to the city council. Once the elections passed, the council seemed inclined to ignore the new committee, but the latter took on a life of its own and began making charges in the press against the city council and the Planning and Zoning Board. The survey was requested by the Citizens Advisory Committee and funded, reluctantly, by the city council.

Delray Beach was not a case of city government dominated by developers making decisions in opposition to the preferences of most residents. To the contrary, in promoting large-scale commercial development within the city, the city council was pursuing a policy of improving the tax base so as to keep taxes low while also trying to expand the economic opportunities of the area's poorest residents. Until recently, this policy was probably widely supported by most residents, especially the large number of poor blacks living near the city center. Moreover, as we shall see, it was not current conditions that caused public concern. Delray Beach was a city that feared the future because it anticipated overdevelopment. In all likelihood, the source of this fear was the alarm being sounded by the Citizens Advisory Council and other top leaders outside the city government.

Land Use Regulation

At the time of the survey, a large majority of the Delray Beach public supported stronger land use regulation. Sixty-two percent of the respondents in the survey said land use regulations should be strengthened. Twenty percent wanted regulations left as they are. Only 8 percent said that regulations should be relaxed.

Table 5-5. Are the Following "Big Problems"?

	Yes (%)	No (%)	Not sure (%)	Total (%)	N
Run-down areas	79	17	7	100	434
Traffic	59	38	3	100	434
Crime	59	35	6	100	434
Loss of open space	53	34	13	100	434
Buildings in residential areas	42	48	10	100	434
Cost of housing	34	49	17	100	434

Support for strengthening land use regulation was not spread evenly throughout the population. Support for stronger controls on development was greatest in the middle- and upper-class neighborhoods in the western and eastern borders of the city. (Support for stronger regulation was also greatest among females, homeowners rather than renters, those with higher levels of education and income, and those who have lived in the city at least three years but fewer than twenty.) The central area, which is predominantly black and poor, did not have a majority in favor of stronger regulation.

By now we have learned to look for the factors that underlie public support for land use controls. In the case of Delray Beach, a number of findings suggest that it was concern about commercial development and automobile traffic.

Perceptions of Problems

At the time of the survey, residents of Delray Beach did not appear to believe that the city's population growth was hurting the area's quality of life. Respondents were asked whether in their view the quality of life in Delray Beach was getting better, getting worse, or not changing.[11] Almost half (46 percent) of the respondents said that the quality of life was not changing. Twenty-eight percent felt that it was getting better, and 24 percent that it was getting worse.

Even though city residents said that the quality of life generally was remaining stable, they perceived a number of specific problems. Respondents were asked a series of questions about whether they would rate certain issues as "big problems" in Delray Beach.[12] In table 5-5 are listed the issues in rank order based on the responses that were given. The most common complaint was the run-down condition of some areas of the city. More than three-fourths (76 percent) of the respondents said that this was a big problem. Next came traffic and crime, each cited by 59 percent of the sample. The remaining issue seen by a majority (53 percent) as a big problem was the loss of open space.

Residents found two other issues less troublesome: the cost of housing and the location of buildings for businesses in residential areas. Less than half of the respondents rated these as big problems. We shall see that this lack of concern at the present time about office buildings contrasted starkly with what the public expected for the future.

The first hint that Delray Beach residents anticipated some changes came from a question that followed up the questions on the city's "big problems." Respondents were asked which of the problems discussed above would be the city's worst problem five years from now. Almost half (42 percent) said traffic. The two next most frequently cited problems were crime (25 percent) and loss of open space (15 percent).

Office Buildings

Consistent with their fears about traffic, city residents were very concerned about adding new office buildings within the city. First of all, they were divided over whether even to allow any new buildings. More than a third (36 percent) of the respondents said that no new buildings should be constructed. About a quarter (27 percent) said that new buildings should be allowed, and another quarter (29 percent) said that buildings should be allowed only under certain conditions.[13]

Second, even those residents who favored additional buildings had reservations if the buildings were to be in or near residential areas.[14] Respondents who said that the city should allow new buildings were asked if they would still feel that way if the buildings were in or near neighborhoods. More than one-fourth (28 percent) said that in such circumstances they would be opposed to new buildings, and 39 percent said they would favor them only under certain circumstances.

Finally, respondents were strongly in favor of keeping strict limits on the height of new buildings in the city. Sixty-one percent of the respondents said that buildings taller than four stories should not be allowed under any circumstances.[15] Opposition to taller buildings was spread diffusely in the population. A plurality in every demographic grouping, and a majority in most, opposed taller buildings under all conditions.

The Visibility Principle

Sunrise, Lee County, and Delray Beach can be placed on two related continua. One has as its criterion the extent to which new development departs from the existing pattern. All three communities were growing rapidly, but the kind of growth each was experiencing varied widely. Sunrise was simply getting more of the same. At the other extreme, Delray Beach was being transformed from a residential city into a center of commerce and business. In the middle, Lee County was a rural area with an urbanizing coastline and some inland suburban sprawl.

The other continuum along which the three communities are arrayed involves elite reactions to urban growth, ranging from support or indifference to opposition. In Sunrise, top leaders more or less ignored the growth issue because they were proccupied with charges of political corruption. In Lee County, elites were divided and polarized. And in Delray Beach they were leaning toward opposition to growth, at least if it involved large-scale commercial development.

These continua appear to be intertwined. When development does not depart from existing patterns, elites can ignore it. When it is extremely different and problematic, they are inclined to coalesce against it. And when it is moderately different they tend to disagree, some thinking it is beneficial to the economy and others arguing that it will harm the environment or quality of life.

Each of these patterns of land development and elite discourse was associated with a configuration of public opinion that mirrored the positions of top leaders. Sunrise residents appeared to be highly satisfied with the city's quality of life. Residents did not think that the city had many "big problems"; generally they said that the existing level of public facilities and services was adequate; and they believed that land use regulation should be left about as it is now. Thus, even though the city had experienced very rapid growth, the nature of the city's development—primarily upper-middle-class residential—and the lack of concern by public officials kept growth from generating controversy and conflict. The only group that seemed concerned about land use issues was composed of people who had lived in the city for a very long time.

At the other extreme on the continua, the city of Delray Beach was also characterized by a considerable amount of consensus in its public opinion. Residents were not particularly concerned with population growth per se, but rather with the intensity of development and the automobile traffic they expected it to generate. Because of outcries by community leaders, the community was in general agreement that commercial development might lead to overloaded public facilities, and residents overwhelmingly supported tighter regulation of land use and limitations on the height of buildings. The only people who took a different view of things were the central-city poor.

The most conflictual public opinion was observed in Lee County, which was situated toward the middle of the continua and had both disparate land uses and divided elites. In Lee County, public opinion about the county government's regulation of construction and development was polarized. Compared to their perceptions of other units of government, residents' views of the county government tended to be that it was regulating development either too little or too much; there was not much middle ground. The proregulation group was concerned about environmental protection, while the antiregulation group focused on economic development. This polarization of opinion appeared to have been generated by the nature of new development in the area and by the positions taken by well-known environmentalists and developers. New construction was not enough like existing development to be generally acceptable to most residents, nor was it different and threatening enough to cause either elites or the public to unite in opposition to it.

Overall, then, the pace of population growth has less effect on public opinion than the nature of the development associated with growth and the reactions to it by top leaders. When the pattern of land use remains fairly constant, population growth is unlikely to cause political conflicts or to stimulate an antigrowth sentiment at either the mass or elite levels. Conversely, when new development departs extensively from the existing pattern of land use, leaders and citizens are likely to coalesce in opposition. Environmental publics polarize, and political conflict is likely to be most intense when the new development associated with population growth is moderately different from the existing pattern of land use.

This relationship between the nature of new development and the configuration of environmental publics suggests that, at an individual level, perception is governed by a visibility principle. The more construction and development depart from the existing pattern of land use, the more likely is any individual to reach a negative judgment about growth and change. Development that is only moderately different from the status quo divides the public because some people notice it and become alarmed while others ignore it or at least anticipate no harm. By the same logic, people who have lived in an area for a long time are more likely to recognize change and to oppose it than are people who have little experience against which to evaluate the situation. In short, for the mass public "seeing is believing," but not very much is seen. It takes a dramatic change and strong statements by elites to get most people's attention.

6
Evaluating Options and Tradeoffs

IT IS GENERALLY RECOGNIZED that environmental worries do not lead automatically to support for environmental policies, but the exact nature of the relationship between the public's environmental concerns and its political preferences has not been determined. A widely accepted but nevertheless questionable premise is that policy preferences simply reflect an *attenuation* of underlying concerns. According to the theory, the public's desire to correct environmental problems is restricted or reduced insofar as the correction is perceived to entail costs.

From the point of view of public officials, the validity of this theory is probably the most important question for research on environmental opinion, for leaders must deal with the electorate's preferences as a whole rather than with individual wishes in isolation. Correcting environmental degradation is certainly a popular aim when considered in a vacuum, but in actual practice it must be assessed against other, equally favored objectives. What if environmental policies entail costs in the form of higher taxes or reduced economic activity? The attenuation theory implies that in such instances leaders should moderate their support for environmental protection. On the other hand, if the theory is inaccurate, officials who back away from a tough environmental stance risk being out of step with their constituents.

The attenuation theory has been proposed in two different contexts. One application of it is with respect to the public's apparent unwillingness to pay for orderly, environmentally sensitive development.

Although citizens want public facilities kept abreast of population growth, they often balk when it comes to paying the higher taxes that effective growth management requires (Citrin, 1979; Peretz, 1982). It is not coincidental that the tax revolt has been concentrated in high-growth states such as California and Florida.

The other area where an attenuation theory has been employed is in explaining opposition to noxious public facilities such as airports and landfills. It is often assumed that public facility siting is controversial because many people have a "not-in-my-backyard," or NIMBY, mentality.[1] According to this application of the theory, residents generally favor the construction of new roads, jails, airports, landfills, and the like, but they turn against them if plans are made to locate them close by. The theory is also implicit in the humorous acronym "LULUs," which stands for "locally unwanted land uses."

However, despite its popularity the attenuation theory of environmental attitudes has both conceptual and evidential inadequacies. Conceptually, the theory fails to take into account the diverse ways in which people could approach environmental policies. Some individuals may indeed worry most about the policies' costs, narrowly defined. But there are many other factors that could reasonably be brought to bear in reaching a judgment. A policy's fairness, its implications for related policies, and its effects on the rights of property owners are just a few of the alternative considerations that might be included in the public's deliberations.

The theory's weakness with respect to evidence is that most of the research on this question is quite crude. The usual technique is to ask people how much they are willing to pay in taxes, fees, or other costs for different policies. But this approach provides information only on the relative weighting people attach to different environmental concerns; it tells us nothing about how their preferences are bundled or how the weighting itself was arrived at. For example, even if it were found that people are willing to pay more for protection against pollution than for other types of environmental controls, this could be because they doubt the efficacy of low-cost alternatives such as regulation; or because their personal health is of more concern to them than wildlife protection; or because they think correcting pollution is more costly than dealing with other environmental problems.

A more effective way to get at the public's conception of policy tradeoffs is to examine real-world cases where people are confronted with tough choices. Two such studies are presented in this chapter. One involves a tax limitation measure, and the other focuses on the siting of noxious public facilities. Both studies were conducted in Palm Beach County.

The Fiscal Calculus

The tax limitation was Proposition 1, a proposed amendment to Florida's constitution that would have drastically reduced the taxing powers of state and local governments.[2] In April 1983, Proposition 1 was placed by voter initiative on the November 1984 ballot. Until it was declared unconstitutional by the Florida Supreme Court in April 1984, it was an important topic of public debate.

Proposition 1

Proposition 1 was far more restrictive than the fiscal limitations either proposed or passed in other states. It limited the revenues of all taxing units in the state to their 1980–81 levels with adjustments only for new construction and two-thirds of the rate of inflation. Also, property tax revenues could not increase more than 5 percent from one year to the next. Property taxes on new construction and revenues from the federal government were excluded from the limit, and local governments could exceed the limit for a two-year period given passage of a referendum to fund a specific project. The revenue restriction applied to state government, cities, counties, school districts, hospital districts, and all other units of government with the power to impose taxes. Moreover, as defined by the proposed amendment, revenues included not only taxes but also receipts from licenses and permits, intergovernmental transfers, user fees, court awards, fines, pension fund earnings, profits from the sale of assets, and virtually all other sources of income (deHaven-Smith, 1984b).

Proposition 1 would have had large fiscal impacts in both the short and long run because it did not include adjustments for population growth. With about 200,000 persons moving into the state each year, revenues from driver's licenses, toll roads, water and sewer services, library cards, and all other activities supported by fees grow accordingly. However, because Proposition 1 restricted all revenues, any growth revenues of this type in excess of two-thirds of the inflation rate had to be matched by reductions in revenues from other sources.

In a widely publicized study, Florida's Joint Legislative Management Committee estimated the fiscal impacts of Proposition 1 at the state level. The gap between the Proposition 1 limit and the state revenues officially forecasted for fiscal year 1985–86 (when, if passed, the amendment would have taken effect) was $2.4 billion, a 22.6 percent reduction (Zingale, 1984). Evidencing the long-term implications of the proposed amendment, the study concluded that if Proposition 1 had been adopted ten years earlier, state government revenues for fiscal year 1983–84 would have been less than half the revenues actually received in that year (Consensus Estimating Conference, 1983, p. 11).

In another study, the Florida Advisory Council on Intergovernmental Relations calculated the first-year impact of Proposition 1 on local governments. There would have been considerable variation across localities because cities and counties vary in population growth and in their reliance on taxes, fees, and federal grants. Rapidly growing areas in the southern part of the state, where Palm Beach County is located, would have experienced some of the greatest first-year reductions. The revenues of the Palm Beach County government would have been reduced by 16.6 percent in the amendment's first year (Florida Advisory Council on Intergovernmental Relations, 1984, p. 157).

The Nature of Tax-Related Belief Systems

Aggregate public opinion on Proposition 1 was similar to what has been observed on fiscal limitations in other states. At the time of the survey, the Palm Beach County public was almost evenly divided on the proposed amendment. Forty-seven percent of the respondents planned to vote against the proposed amendment, while 42 percent said they would vote for it.[3] (The rest were undecided.) Support was strongest among conservatives, individuals with either very high or relatively low incomes, and those fifty-fifty to sixty-five years old. Opposition was concentrated among Democrats, respondents with children in the public schools, and households with government employees.[4]

Two approaches were used to observe how respondents evaluated Proposition 1. One was designed to identify the main factor respondents used in deciding whether to support or oppose the proposition. The other measure assessed the extent to which respondents' positions on Proposition 1 were based on judgments about how budget reductions affected specific public services.

Levels of Conceptualization. The measure used to identify the central

Table 6-1. Positions on Proposition 1 by Levels of Conceptualization

	For (%)	Against (%)	Undecided (%)	All respondents (%)
Ideological	36	18	5	24
Interest-oriented	35	52	27	43
No issue content	29	30	68	33
Total	100	100	100	100
N	(173)	(196)	(37)	(406)

factor respondents used in evaluating the amendment was an adaptation of the approach developed by Converse (1964). Respondents with a position on Proposition 1 were asked what led them to it, and those undecided were asked what kind of information would influence their votes.[5] Respondents were classified into one of three categories depending on their responses. They were categorized as ideological if, in evaluating the amendment, they referred to how it would affect abstract aspects of government, such as its scope, efficiency, responsiveness, or capabilities. Those who evaluated Proposition 1 in terms of its effects on the taxes they pay or the services they receive, effects that are relatively concrete and "close to home," were labeled as interest-oriented. The remaining respondents were classified as having no issue content and included those who could not think of anything to say, who wanted to "send a message" to government, who wanted to just give Proposition 1 a try, or who did not want to tinker with the Florida Constitution.

Across the support, opposition, and undecided cohorts, there was considerable variation in the conceptual basis from which Proposition 1 was evaluated. Conceptual levels are crosstabulated by positions on the amendment in table 6-1. Supporters of the amendment included a comparatively large percentage of ideologues, mainly respondents who thought Proposition 1 would reduce the size of government or increase its efficiency. In contrast, most of those against the amendment had an interest orientation and evaluated it in terms of its effects on taxes and services. Those undecided were seldom able to articulate what kind of information would influence their views.

Service Preferences and Expectations. To assess the extent to which positions on Proposition 1 were based on judgments about its impacts on specific public services and facilities, respondents were asked how they would want Florida's governments to handle various responsibilities in

Table 6-2. Correlations (Gammas) between Service Preferences and Expectations

	Supporters,			Opponents,				
	Ideo-logues	Interest-oriented	No issue content	Ideo-logues	interest-oriented	No issue content	Unde-cided	Total sample
Education	.157	.129	−.062	−.538*	−.217*	.075	−.137	−.087*
Road construction and maintenance	.054	.054*	.295	−.141	.055	.093	.333	.199*
Parks and recreation	.295	.451*	.295	.159	.133	.191	.477	.267*
Utilities	.324*	.052	.094	.626*	.213*	.146	.283	.217*
Aid to the poor	.394*	.183	.352*	.017	−.191*	−.069*	.544*	.154*
Administrative personnel	.170	.468*	.290	.329*	.288*	.119	−.352	.142*
N	(55–62)	(56–61)	(42–45)	(36–37)	(91–100)	(51–56)	(29–40)	(363–400)

*Chi square significant at .05 or better.

the event of a major budget reduction, and also what they would actually expect Florida's government to do.[6] In table 6-2 are listed the correlations (Gammas) between preferences and expectations for respondents broken down by their positions on Proposition 1 and their levels of conceptualization.[7] Generally, negative correlations would be anticipated for opponents of the amendment, because their expectations about how Proposition 1 would affect services should be contrary to their desires. Conversely, positive correlations would be predicted for the supporters. A correlation near zero indicates that preferences and expectations are largely independent and hence are not part of respondents' evaluations of the proposed fiscal limitation.

Respondents did indeed evaluate Proposition 1 in terms of its service impacts, but the services varied across levels of conceptualization and positions on the amendment (table 6-2). Belief systems at the lowest level of conceptualization had the least content regarding the effects of the fiscal limitation on specific services. Among respondents with no issue content in their evaluations of Proposition 1, only one of the relationships between preferences and expectations was statistically significant. Crosstabulations (not shown) revealed that these respondents, regardless of whether they supported Proposition 1, tended to prefer that services be left as they are and seldom expected budget cuts to cause service reductions. As might be expected, respondents in this group had a low level of education in comparison to the rest of the sample.

Ideological supporters of Proposition 1 focused on utilities and aid to the poor. For both services, cuts were favored and expected by about one-third of the group, with most others in the group expecting and preferring the services to remain the same. The low correlation on administrative personnel, which appears inconsistent with this group's desire to reduce the size of government and increase its efficiency, stemmed from a conclusion that budget cuts will not reduce public employment for management and record keeping. Almost two-thirds of the ideological supporters wanted cuts in administrative personnel, but only half actually expected cuts and more than 20 percent expected increases. This group tended to be middle-aged and to be toward the low end of the income scale (although not below $10,000 annual income).

Interest-oriented supporters of Proposition 1 had highly correlated preferences and expectations on administrative personnel, parks and recreation, and road construction and maintenance. Of all the belief systems under analysis, this one most closely corresponded to the pattern of service impacts expected by Proposition 1's designers. The amendment's designers wanted to force Florida's governments to focus on such essential services as public safety, health care, and aid to the poor, and either curtail their other activities or finance them separately with user-charges. Interest-oriented supporters of Proposition 1 tended to be quite well off financially in comparison to the rest of the sample.

In contrast to Proposition 1's supporters, opponents of the amendment focused mainly on the impacts they expected a budget cut to have on educational services. Together, opponents at the ideological and interest-oriented levels of conceptualization had three statistically significant, positive correlations between their preferences and expectations on services outside the education area. For all three correlations, cuts were favored and expected. Apparently, these respondents planned to vote against Proposition 1 because, even though they found service reductions in several areas acceptable, the unwanted reductions they expected in education were an overriding consideration. Faced with a hypothetical reduction in government budgets, more than two-thirds of the ideological and interest-oriented opponents of Proposition 1 wanted expenditures for education to be increased, but more than half of the respondents in both groups expected education funding to be cut. This group tended to be middle-class young adults with children.

Finally, respondents who were undecided also had mixed evaluations. They favored the reductions they expected on most services but were opposed to cuts in administrative personnel and education. Presumably, how this group would have voted would have depended on the relative importance it attached to different public services.

In the Eye of the Beholder

Our discoveries about public opinion on Proposition 1 are similar to our findings on issues of land use regulation and environmental protection. Public opinion on Proposition 1 was grounded in diverse orientations. Some saw it as a way to reduce taxes; some focused on the services they might lose; some viewed the amendment as an antidote to government expansion and inefficiency; and some had no issue content at all in their positions.

Even when people agreed in evaluating the amendment against its effects on public services, the services considered important varied from one group to the next. Although supporters of Proposition 1 were not decidedly negative about any of the service impacts they expected from budget cuts, the ideological and interest-oriented components of the support coalition based their evaluations of the fiscal limitation on opposite sets of services. Conversely, Proposition 1's opponents did not prefer the reductions in education that they thought the amendment would require, but they favored some of the service reductions they expected budget cuts to cause in other areas.

The NIMBY Syndrome

Data for a study of public opinion toward noxious public facilities came from a telephone survey administered in Palm Beach County between March and April 1987. Although a variety of facilities was covered, the survey focused particularly on a number of road improvements that had been opposed by neighborhood groups representing nearby homeowners. Six separate samples were drawn—one for the county as a whole, and five others from "catchment areas" around the controversial road projects.[8] The five catchment areas were: (1) south county around southeast Eighteenth Street; (2) Lake Ida Road; (3) Woolbright Road; (4) a proposed east-west expressway from West Palm Beach on the coast inland to Royal Palm Beach; and (5) north county around Center Street, Hood Road, and Prosperity Farms Road. Each catchment area as well as the countywide sample included at least one hundred completed interviews.

The catchment area boundaries were defined along zip code lines because the listing of telephone numbers from which the samples were drawn provided zip codes as a geographical reference. To the extent possible given the use of zip codes, the boundaries were delineated to capture those residents who were likely to experience at least some inconveniences from the road improvements while excluding those who would benefit without having to experience any offsetting annoyances. A map of the county showing the catchment areas is provided in figure 6-1.

The survey included three types of questions. First, there were two questions that asked whether the county government should proceed with the construction of a road or a "trashfill" even if neighborhoods in the vicinity would be harmed.[9] A second set of questions dealt with several proposed facilities—a new airport, road linkages with the county to the south, and a major expressway extension—that would affect the entire county but that were only at the planning stages.[10] Both this and the first set of questions were asked for all six samples. A third group of questions focused on the projects in the five catchment areas. Respondents in each catchment area were asked whether or not the county government should proceed with the road project(s) slated for their particular area.[11]

Findings

Public opinion varied toward the LULUs covered in the survey, depending on the type of project involved (table 6-3). A plurality of the respondents opposed only two projects. One was the proposed east-west expressway linking the city of West Palm Beach to an inland suburb. The other project concerned a "trashfill" where the site was not specified.

Why these particular projects generated public opposition is not evident from the aggregate data shown in table 6-3. It could be, as the attenuation and NIMBY theories imply, that more people are harmed

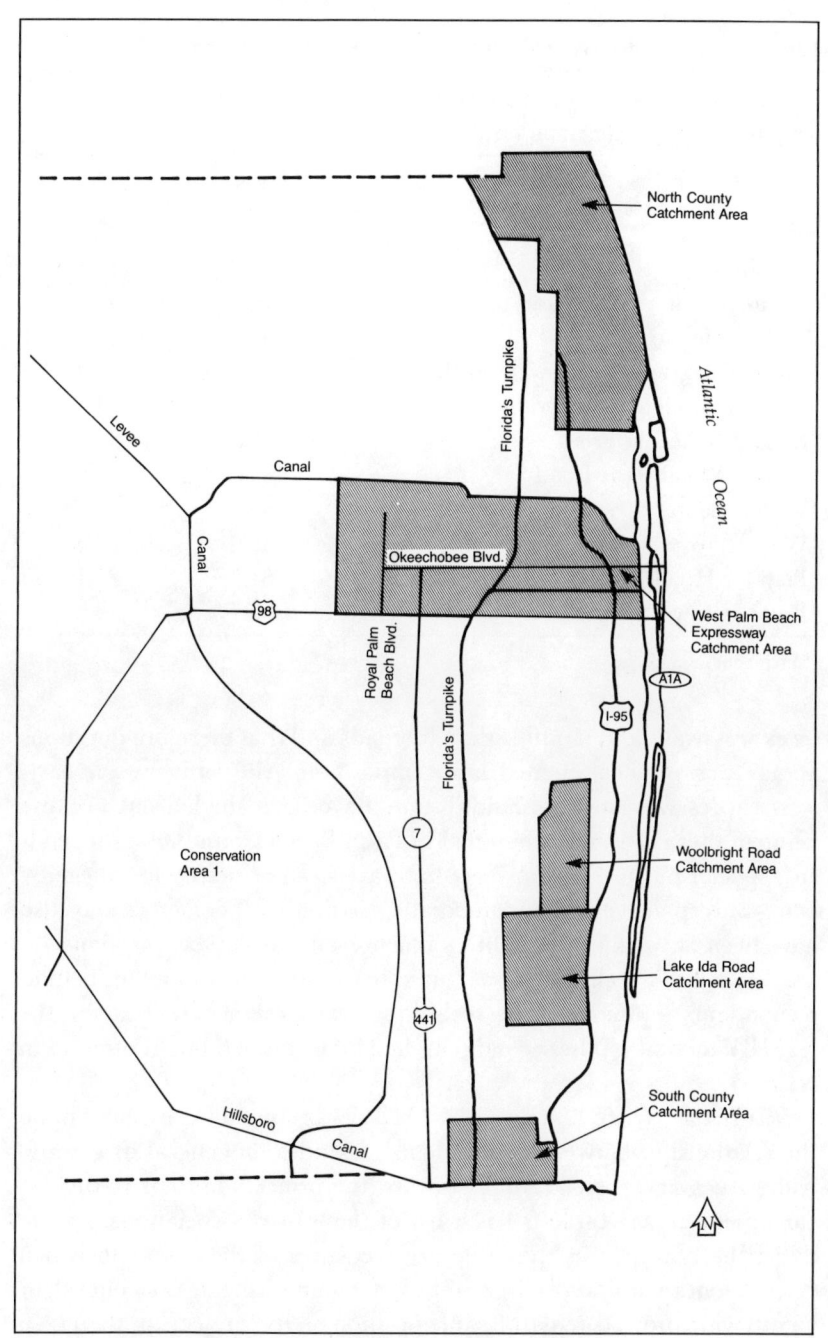

Figure 6.1. County Catchment Areas

Table 6-3. Attitudes toward Different Palm Beach County LULUs

Should the following projects be undertaken even if nearby neighborhoods are harmed or alarmed?

	Yes	No
Roads in general	60.7	17.0
A trashfill	35.5	42.7
New airport in north county	48.6	33.9
Road linkage to Broward	56.9	34.9
Extend Sawgrass expressway north	57.8	33.0
*Build S.W. eighteenth bridge	70.8	18.6
*Extend Lake Ida Road	55.3	30.1
*Extend Woolbright Road	82.5	10.5
*Widen Center Street	62.9	16.5
*Widen Prosperity Farms	66.0	26.8
*Plan for Hood Road	61.5	27.1
*Build east-west expressway	39.7	46.6

*Catchment area sample

by expressways and landfills than by roads and that therefore questions about such projects elicited more opposition. Alternatively, the east-west expressway and the landfill may have been singled out because siting of these facilities is handled in Palm Beach County by independent, special purpose authorities that have been criticized for allegedly being unresponsive and undemocratic. No doubt other factors may also have been at work in the public's reactions to the survey questions.

Two analytic techniques were used to examine the rationales behind respondents' opinions. One technique was designed to test for the NIMBY mentality; the second searched for forms of thought other than NIMBY.

The Test for NIMBY. A test for NIMBY was conducted by examining the relationship between respondents' attitudes on general or county-wide issues and their attitudes toward the projects in their particular catchment areas. Table 6-4 is a list of the Tau-B associations. Essentially, the numbers in the table are measures of the extent to which respondents who favored or opposed moving ahead on general or countywide projects took the same position on the projects in their own areas. If a NIMBY mentality were widespread, most of the Tau-B

Table 6-4. Tau-B Associations between General Attitudes and Attitudes toward Catchment Area Road Projects

	Build roads	Build landfill	Build airport	Road links to next county	Extend Sawgrass Expressway
South County	.10	.07	−.05	.18*	.22*
Lake Ida	.23*	.01	.20*	.17*	.07
Woolbright	.34*	.06	.17*	.21*	.14
West Palm Beach Expressway	.21*	.06	.01	.16*	.33*
Hood Road	.01	.21*	.20*	.11	.12
Center Street	.07	−.08	.25*	.21*	.08
Prosperity Farm	.18	−.11	.19	.26*	.33*

associations would be negative, indicating support for public facilities in general but opposition when they are close by.

Almost all of the associations are positive, and those dealing exclusively with roads or expressways are usually large and statistically significant. This does not mean that a NIMBY orientation is totally absent, only that it is not as widespread as might have been expected. Crosstabs (not shown) reveal that even when the Tau-B is higher than .2, as many as 36 percent of the respondents who favor a project in the abstract oppose the particular project in their own catchment area.

The implication of table 6-4 is simply that NIMBY is not the only form of thinking associated with the county's LULUs. In contrast to those who worried only about their own backyards, some people consistently favored new facilities, while other people consistently opposed them, regardless of what kind of facilities were at issue or where they would be located. In the next section some of the concerns underlying these non-NIMBY response patterns are discussed.

Issue Publics. The effort to identify forms of thought other than NIMBY began by dividing the sample into issue publics. During the survey, respondents were asked an open-ended question about what issue they thought was most pressing for the county.[12] Four concerns were common: traffic; population growth and urbanization; crime and other social problems; and poor government.

In table 6-5 respondents have been divided according to the problem

Table 6-5. Attitudes of Different Issue Publics

Biggest problem	Traffic	Growth	Crime, etc.	Poor government	Grand mean	N
Roads in general	4	−9	5	−2	25	(433)
A trashfill	4	−10	4	9	20	(422)
New airport in north county	4	−3	−1	−2	22	(446)
Next county road links	6	−9	−2	−3	23	(449)
Extend Sawgrass	5	−10	7	−9	23	(448)
S.W. 18th Bridge	5	−12	—	5	25	(053)
Lake Ida Road	5	−8	—	5	24	(059)
Woolbright Road	−1	1	—	1	27	(050)
Center Street	0	−4	4	2	25	(058)
Prosperity Farms	2	−5	5	−2	24	(058)
Hood Road	3	−6	−2	−9	23	(057)
East-west expressway	8	−9	9	0	20	(070)

that most worried them, and the various questions about public facilities have been coded 10 for opposition, 20 for "not sure," and 30 for support. The numbers in the table are deviations from an overall average for the question under analysis. Given that the grand mean can never be less than 10 or greater than 30, deviations from the mean can range from −20 to 20. Negative numbers indicate more opposition than average to the project or facility, while positive numbers indicate more support than average.

The figures in table 6-5 suggest that residents' concerns about the county significantly influenced their positions toward public facilities. People who were worried mainly about traffic consistently favored expanding the county's infrastructure. This was true not only with regard to road projects but also in their attitudes toward the landfill and the new airport. In every instance except the questions pertaining to Woolbright Road and Center Street, respondents in this group were more likely on average to support construction of the LULU than were respondents with other concerns.

Conversely, those who were worried about population growth and urbanization consistently opposed the projects covered in the survey.

The one exception to this pattern was Woolbright Road. On all of the other projects—again including the landfill and the airport—this group was decidedly negative.

Finally, the issue publics focusing on social problems and government did not have consistent attitudes one way or the other on the LULUs covered by the survey. Presumably because they were not very concerned about issues related to the county's population growth, their responses to the survey questions depended on other factors. It was probably in these groups that the NIMBY mentality was most common.

There is More to LULUs Than NIMBY

Public opinion in Palm Beach County suggests that there is more to conflict over LULUs than a not-in-my-backyard mentality. The NIMBY theory assumes that controversies surrounding LULUs stem simply from real or perceived threats to health, safety, and property. The possibility that there might be issues at stake other than localized risks is not considered.

In contradiction to the NIMBY model, Palm Beach countians evaluated LULUs from a variety of perspectives. Many respondents favored road projects even though the projects were located close to them and were designed mainly to serve people outside their immediate areas. Their support appears to have been based in part on an overriding desire to reduce traffic. Conversely, many residents opposed new facilities even though they themselves would not necessarily be threatened by the facilities' locations. Hostile to the county's urbanization and perhaps hoping to limit it by restricting the provision of infrastructure, people in this group opposed new roads and other extensions of infrastructure even when projects were far away. To be sure, some of the county's residents had a not-in-my-backyard philosophy, but NIMBY was only one of several points of view.

Although it is possible that concerns other than risk and issues other than siting were evident in Palm Beach County because of the nature of the LULUs considered, there are several reasons for believing that the study's findings are applicable to LULUs generally. In Palm Beach County the attitudes of the antigrowth and antitraffic publics extended not only to roads but also to airports and landfills. This suggests that, at least within limits, an increase in the scale of LULUs or a shift in the nature of their impact does not necessarily trigger a NIMBY reaction. Moreover, it is easy to imagine circumstances where concerns other than personal safety would be considered by host communities even if the public facilities in question posed extremely high risks. A very poor community might view a hazardous waste disposal facility as a source of jobs. Similarly, how residents would evaluate a proposed nuclear power facility might depend in part on their attitudes toward technology and modernization.

Environmental Publics and Coalition Politics

The two studies presented in this chapter show that just as people's environmental concerns are very mundane and diverse, their assessments of policy tradeoffs are rooted in a variety of narrowly focused perspectives. For mnemonic purposes we can refer to this as the principle of overriding interests. How people assess a proposed reduction in public services, a controversial landfill, or a nearby road project depends on the things that are most important to them, usually in their everyday life. For some it is schools for their children or traveling to work with minimal delays. For others it is taxes, population growth, or something else. Policy proposals are evaluated in terms of how they affect these overriding considerations.

The principle of overriding interests has at least two important implications. First, it means that the relationship between people's environmental concerns and their positions on environmental policy is not so much attenuated as it is splintered and variegated. People may recognize that environmental problems are occurring in their area, and as long as the options are presented to them in a vacuum (as in a public opinion survey), they may be very supportive of environmental protection. But when they are confronted with a real-life policy, they will evaluate it in light of its effects on issues related to their circumstances and lifestyles. Since social conditions vary tremendously, the conclusions that different people reach will be quite diverse.

Second, the principle of overriding interests implies that coalitions on growth management and environmental protection will be relatively fluid. In theory, coalitions will shift depending on how a proposed policy is seen to affect various issues of concern among the community. On one hand, this opens up the possibility for broadening support for proposals that may be controversial. For example, the NIMBY syndrome can be mitigated by arguments that noxious public facilities are necessary for economic growth or smooth traffic flow. On the other hand, however, it means that environmental coalitions are difficult to hold together in the face of visible costs or drawbacks. Many people may initially endorse a proposed policy of environmental protection but quickly withdraw their support if it harms other things they value more. In the next chapter, this process of coalition disintegration is examined in detail.

7
Environmental Publics in Motion

THUS FAR WE HAVE considered the components of environmental opinion separately and in isolation. Environmental concerns have been found to be locally oriented, narrowly focused, and crudely conceptualized, while the factors that intervene between concern and action are numerous and diverse. The question that arises at this point is how these components operate together in a dynamic political context.

This chapter is a case study of environmental opinion under stress. The study charts the changes that occurred in environmental attitudes as the Area of Critical State Concern program was implemented in the Florida Keys. In order to protect local natural resources, the program imposed significant and widespread costs on the population. Thus it provided a setting for answering how environmental concerns, political judgments, and elite discourse interact to shape aggregate opinion.

Data for the study came from four surveys: three public opinion surveys and a survey of residents who owned undeveloped lots in the Keys. The public opinion surveys were conducted in the fall of 1984, 1985, and 1986. The lot owner survey was run in December 1985.[1]

Regulating Paradise

The Keys are a string of islands running from the southern tip of mainland Florida about 120 miles into the ocean toward Cuba. Most of the islands are long and narrow—only a mile or two wide at most. The surrounding ocean is usually calm and clear and is internationally known for its abundant sea life. Linked together by a long, two-lane highway and a series of bridges, the Keys look from the air like a string of green and pink beads floating in shallow, blue water.

History of State Activities

Population growth in the Keys since the 1970s has not been particularly rapid in comparison to the growth experienced in other areas of the state (see Appendix, table 1), but it has occurred faster than the ecologically fragile and geographically narrow islands can handle. The Keys comprise roughly the entire geographical area of Monroe County. The county's population expanded from 52,586 in 1970 to 68,752 in 1984 (*Florida Statistical Abstract*, 1985, table 1.67, p. 26). Not counted in these figures are thousands of additional residents who own property in the Keys but live there only a few months each year. Many of the islands are now overdeveloped with condominiums; traffic congestion on the two-lane, north-south highway is a serious problem; and public services, particularly wastewater treatment and solid waste disposal, barely meet the population's needs.

Since the mid-1970s, Florida's state government has been working with regional and local agencies in the Keys to protect the area's fragile environment. The Florida Keys were designated as an Area of Critical State Concern (ACSC) in 1975. In large part this action was opposed by local elected and appointed officials, and by many civic leaders as well. They viewed the designation as unnecessary interference in Monroe County affairs, and they were also concerned about the designation's potential effects on the local economy. Litigation followed, and in 1978 the Florida Supreme Court held that the ACSC program was unconstitutional on the grounds that the state legislature unlawfully delegated its authority to an administrative agency.

In 1979 the legislature responded to the court's ruling in three ways. First, it legislatively redesignated the Keys as an ACSC. Second, it resolved the unlawful delegation problem in the ACSC program by requiring legislative review of ACSC administrative designations. And third, it strengthened the ACSC program by mandating that the governor appoint resource planning and management committees in designated Areas of Critical State Concern and areas being considered for designation. In areas already designated, the resource planning and management committees were assigned the responsibility of monitoring local implementation of land use regulations.

A resource planning and management committee was appointed in the Keys in 1981. The governor instructed the committee to review the land use regulations of the county and municipal governments and determine if the regulations and their implementation met the requirements for repeal of the Keys' ACSC designation. To handle these tasks the Keys' resource planning and management committee formed a technical advisory committee, which, after careful study, reached these conclusions:

> standards and guidelines for land use decisions in the Keys were insufficient to meet the ACSC principles for development;
> because of understaffing, the local planning and zoning departments were unable to enforce existing standards;
> local zoning boards and county commissioners did not take the existing standards seriously; and
> the state had failed to staff its offices with sufficient personnel to monitor implementation and enforce ACSC requirements.

The report of the resource planning and management committee along with a series of articles by the state's leading newspaper (the *Miami Herald*) generated public alarm. One new county commissioner was elected in November 1982 and another in 1984 running on platforms of growth management. Both were Republicans and were elected despite a two-to-one Democratic advantage among registered voters.

The Comprehensive Plan

The new Comprehensive Plan mandated by the ACSC designation was written and reviewed primarily between 1984 and 1986. Once a draft of the Plan was available, over ninety public hearings were held by the county commission to receive public comment. It is an understatement to say that the Plan was controversial. It was adopted only by a three-to-two vote on the five-member county commission, and no one knew until the very last minute whether the commission would approve it.

The controversy surrounding the Plan centered on how it affected the ability of lot owners to develop their property. During the past fifty years, more than fourteen thousand acres in the Florida Keys were subdivided into almost fifty-three thousand lots, the vast majority for residential use. Approximately thirty-two thousand of these lots remained to be developed. The difficulty the Plan had to address was that the Keys could handle only about twenty thousand more dwelling units given the county's projected ability to provide roads, water and wastewater treatment, and other public facilities.

The proposed Comprehensive Plan divided platted residential lots into two classes: improved subdivisions and unimproved subdivisions. An improved subdivision was defined as a recorded subdivision that had all required improvements in place (or available) including roads, water, electricity and telephone lines. Approximately sixteen thousand lots qualified as improved subdivision lots. Lots in improved subdivisions were allocated a density of one dwelling per lot regardless of size, except that where contiguous lots were in common ownership on the effective date of the Plan, the owner was entitled to only one unit per 12,500 square feet. In contrast, the remaining lots (15,427) were treated as acreage under the Plan, a circumstance that theoretically required the assembly of as many as nine lots to achieve a minimum density of one dwelling unit. Thus the proposed Plan dealt with the Keys' platted subdivision problem by effectively downzoning the entire county. It was a radical solution, but it was the only alternative available given the state's requirements in the Keys' ACSC designation.

The controversy that developed once the proposed Plan was made public is understandable in light of the pattern of lot ownership. The 1985 public opinion survey revealed that 15 percent of all households in the county owned at least one undeveloped lot in the Keys, and the lot owner survey found that the land holdings of two groups—realtors and wealthy residents—were very extensive. At the same time, other lot owners with smaller holdings—one or two lots in a single subdivision— also had reasons to be alarmed. Some of these owners of small parcels expected to make big profits on their investments, while others wanted to build a future residence. The Plan thus presented a roadblock to their intentions as well. In short, somewhere between 10 and 20 percent of the households in the Keys potentially could have been losers under the proposed Plan as a direct result of the Plan's effects on development rights. Added to this pool of discontented property owners were others who, although not directly affected by the Plan, feared that it might dampen the Keys' economic growth and hence deprive them of income indirectly.

In an effort to make the Plan more palatable to local lot owners, the state legislature authorized the county commission to establish a land authority to help lot owners reap some profits from their holdings. The idea was for the land authority to purchase entire subdivisions or sections of subdivisions, redesign the lot layout at a lower density, and then sell the subdivision for development, returning any profits to the original lot owners on a pro rata basis. In principle this process could be used throughout the Keys to spread the costs and benefits of the Plan more evenly across the lot owner population.

The largest source of funding for the land authority was to have been a one-cent sales tax on receipts at tourist attractions. To take effect, the tourist impact tax, as it was called, had to be supported by voters in the November 1986 election. Like the Plan, the tax became embroiled in controversy. Those who opposed it said that the money it would provide was "a crumb" and "a diversion by the state" (quoted in Sigo, 1986, p. 6).

Ultimately, after all of this controversy over the Plan and the proposed tourist impact tax, the public appeared to reverse itself. In November 1986 three new county commissioners were elected—all Democrats who had campaigned on platforms critical of the Plan and of the tax. The only incumbent commissioner who was running—a Republican—had been the Plan's most vocal advocate, and she was defeated. Furthermore, the tourist impact tax was rejected.

A Loss of Environmental Will

As the ACSC program was implemented, residents were confronted with a series of choices that became increasingly concrete and difficult. Initially the issue was simply whether more extensive land use controls were needed. Then came the proposed Comprehensive Plan and finally the land authority and tourist impact tax.

Two approaches were used to examine how public opinion evolved as the policy context narrowed. One approach was to track the evolution of public opinion in the aggregate. This method indicated how knowledge of growth management issues spread, when and at what level public opinion turned against land use controls, and which demographic groups were involved. The second method was to use results from the 1986 survey to investigate how the same individuals responded to all of the policy choices over the three-year period. This approach focused on the issue public concerned with growth management and provided a time-lapse image of its dissolution.

Opinion Trends

A comparison of the 1984, 1985, and 1986 public opinion surveys revealed a sharp disjuncture between attitudes toward growth management issues generally and assessments of the Plan and the tourist impact tax. Opinions on general questions of policy remained relatively supportive of environmental protection throughout the period in question. Two questions were asked in all three surveys. One was whether the natural environment in the Keys was deteriorating.[2] The percentage saying that the environment was getting worse declined slightly from 59 in 1984, to 55 in 1985, and to 50 in 1986. The second question was whether land use controls needed to be strengthened.[3] Again there was only a modest decline in the frequency of attitudes supporting environmental protection. The percentage saying that land use regulations needed to be strengthened declined from 59 to 56 and then to 52 across the three time points.

In contrast to the stability of attitudes toward policy in the abstract, public opinion toward the Comprehensive Plan changed markedly between the time the Plan was introduced in 1985 and the election of 1986. Of the respondents aware of the Plan in 1985, most were uncertain.[4] Twenty-four percent favored the Plan, 30 percent opposed it, and 46 percent had not made up their minds. However, by 1986 the undecided group had declined to 31 percent of the respondents, the supporters had increased only slightly to 29 percent, and the opposition group had become the plurality with 40 percent.

This shift in public opinion toward the Plan appears to have been due to actual changes in attitudes rather than to changes in the number or types of people interested in the topic. In both 1985 and 1986, a little more than 70 percent of the respondents said they had heard of the new Plan. A comparison of the distribution of *awareness* within different demographic groupings found no statistically significant differences between the 1985 and 1986 frequencies. However, a similar demographic comparison of *positions* on the Plan revealed increases in support for the Plan among retirees, government employees, and people who had lived in the Keys less than six years. There were decreases in support for the Plan among lot owners, renters, residents in the tourist and real estate industries, and people who had lived in the Keys longer than six years.

The election outcome of 1986 was not entirely the result of the controversy surrounding the Plan. Only one of the voting decisions in the 1986 election appears to have been influenced by respondents' positions on the Plan—votes on the tourist impact tax.[5] The Tau-B association between attitudes toward the Plan and votes on the tax was .27 (significant at .05). In contrast, the associations between attitudes toward the Plan and votes on candidates for the county commission did not exceed .04.[6] This suggests that, as the growth management issue lost its attraction, people returned to their initial political orientation, that is, to their party of registration.

Overall, then, the public's reaction to the Plan seems to have been highly localized in at least two senses. First, most people's reactions were focused narrowly on the Plan and the tourist impact tax. When residents saw that growth management had high costs, they did not respond by changing their basic posture toward land use regulation or environmental protection, nor did they extend their concerns about the Plan and the tax to their evaluations of the candidates for county commission. Second, public reaction was localized in the sense that the crystallization of opinion toward the Plan that occurred between 1985 and 1986 involved only a few groups. Newcomers, retirees, and government employees swung behind the Plan, while long-time residents, lot owners, and a few other groups jumped to the opposition. Everyone else stuck with their initial position.

The Issue Public

The issue public interested in growth management was identified on the basis of several questions in the 1986 survey. Respondents were classified as belonging to the issue public if they had a position on the question about land use regulation, knew about the Plan, and had voted one way or the other on the tourist impact tax. Thirty-five percent of the sample, or 144 respondents, qualified. Compared to others in the sample, respondents in the issue public were older, better educated, wealthier, and more likely to own undeveloped lots.

The growth management public appears to have contained a number of distinct ideological groupings. Six groupings based on variations in attitudes toward land use regulation, the Plan, and the tourist impact tax are presented in table 7-1. The names for each grouping were developed intuitively on the basis of discussions with area residents and leaders and by reconstructing the ideology that would be expected to underlie each attitude pattern if we hypothesize that voters are reasonable.

The "free enterprisers" are the easiest to understand. Presumably,

Table 7-1. Alternative Orientations to Growth Management Policies in the Keys

	Attitude toward land use regulations	Attitude toward comprehensive plan	Attitude toward impact tax	Frequency (%)
Free enterprise	−	−	−	12
No growthers	+	+	−	23
Weak growth mgrs	+	−	−	19
Strong growth mgrs	+	+	+	32
Environmentalists	+	−	+	10
Progrowthers	−	−	+	4
Total				100
N				(144)

people who think land use regulation should be relaxed, who oppose the Plan, and who voted against the tourist impact tax want unrestricted development. The rationales hypothesized for the other groupings are as follows: "No growthers" want strong limitations on development. They oppose the tourist impact tax because in their view the tax would facilitate construction on lots that are otherwise undeveloped. "Weak growth managers" say that land use regulation needs to be strengthened, but they oppose both the Plan and the tax, suggesting that their support for land use controls is very soft. "Strong growth managers," that is, those who support all three policies, adhere to the ideology of the leaders who developed the Plan and the land authority. "Environmentalists" want strong land use controls and oppose the Plan because in their view it is too weak. They voted for the tax only because they think the Plan is better than nothing, and they see the tax as necessary to mollify the opposition. "Progrowthers" oppose land use restrictions and the Plan, but they favor the tax because they believe that the land authority may help promote growth and development.

Assuming that most people's attitudes toward land use regulation (as a general policy) did not change much over time, table 7-1 provides an overview of how the growth management coalition evolved. The first column is a rough picture of what the coalition looked like in 1984. The plus signs represent those who said land use regulation should either be strengthened or left as it is, while the minus signs represent those who said regulation should be relaxed. At a general level, everyone was in the growth management camp except for the free enterprisers and the progrowthers, who together represented only 16 percent of the sample. The second column shows that two groups emerged and then split off from the growth management coalition as the Comprehensive Plan was developed and debated: the weak growth managers and the environmentalists. The plus signs in this column represent those who were unsure about the Plan, and, hence, when the frequencies are summed the growth management coalition still includes a slim majority. Given that initially most people were uncertain about the Plan and that it took a while for opinion toward the Plan to crystallize, we have reason to believe that the weak growth managers and environmentalists did not really exist as solid ideological groupings (at least not vis-à-vis the Plan) until well into 1985.

Finally, the third column suggests that the defeat of the proposed tourist impact tax involved some strange bedfellows. The tax was rejected by a coalition of free enterprisers, no growthers, and weak growth managers—presumably with each group voting against the tax for a different reason.

Perspectives on the Plan

The 1986 survey included a series of questions covering various aspects of the Plan.[7] The responses of each ideological grouping are shown in table 7-2. The numbers are deviations from the grand mean for each row. Answers were coded "10" for responses critical of the Plan and "20" for responses supportive of the Plan. Thus negative numbers in the table indicate that the group was more negative than average on that particular aspect of the Plan. The largest negative number in each column indicates the particular attitude toward the Plan that most separates the group from the total sample.

Each ideological grouping saw the Plan in a different light. As would be expected, the strong growth managers were least likely to think that the Plan was problematic. Their only concern—and a very slight one at that—appears to have been that the Plan might not provide enough environmental protection. Environmentalists shared this concern, but much more extensively. The weak growth managers differed most from the rest of the population in their view that the Plan would cause housing costs to rise. The no growthers feared that the Plan might allow

Table 7-2. Assessment of Various Aspects of the Plan by Different Ideological Groupings

	Free enterprisers	No growthers	Weak growth managers	Strong growth managers	Environmentalists	Pro-growthers
Impact on the economy	−38	27	−8	27	−9	−51
Limits on property rights	−16	9	−6	23	−8	17
Effects on housing costs	−27	16	−18	25	−2	6
Inadequate environmental protection	22	6	−6	−5	−28	56
Allowing too much development	17	−14	−9	8	−7	10
Plan's fairness	−10	0	−10	23	1	−10
How Plan affects the respondent	−9	7	4	10	−1	−23

too much development, while the progrowthers worried that the Plan would harm the economy and would hurt them personally. Finally, the free enterprisers were concerned most about how the Plan would affect both the economy and the cost of housing.

The Inherent Instability of Environmental Opinion

Public opinion in the Florida Keys during the ACSC planning process shows that the configuration of issue publics in a particular locale is not static. Issue publics will form and reform as conditions change. Because most people's attitudes on environmental issues are focused narrowly on their immediate circumstances rather than being rooted in an abstract philosophy, their attitudes shift as their circumstances change. With regard to environmental conditions, the changes in circumstances and hence in public opinion are usually gradual. In contrast, the political context in which property owners find themselves can change quite rapidly. Proposed policies can divide the public in many different ways, depending on how costs and benefits are distributed and what are the overriding concerns of the citizenry.

In the case of the Comprehensive Plan for the Florida Keys, the coalition that in 1984 favored developing the Plan included people with different (and, in some instances, conflicting) objectives and values. Some people were concerned about the Keys' fragile ecology, others about maintaining a tropical island atmosphere, and still others about the economy or the housing market or both. As the Plan was developed, decisions had to be made about which of these concerns was most important, and this inevitably resulted in some people being pleased and others disappointed. Had a fundamentally different kind of Plan been proposed; had extensive public purchase of undeveloped lots been used as the primary means of preventing overdevelopment; or had the land authority been funded by proceeds from some revenue-source other than a tourist impact tax, the social and ideological makeup of the growth management public would probably have been quite different.

The Comprehensive Plan that was actually proposed ended up alienating many of the Keys' residents because it took a middle course. The coalition that emerged between 1982 and 1984 and that led to the development of the Plan splintered into several ideological groupings as the policy choices narrowed. At one extreme were the "no growthers" and environmentalists, both of whom favored very strict regulations. At the other extreme were the "weak growth managers," whose idea of land use controls seems to have been quite modest. In the middle were the strong growth managers, the people who desired a strict Plan along with some mechanisms to help compensate the lot owners for their losses. The plan that was finally adopted satisfied the moderates but disappointed the extremists on both sides.

8
Environmentalism at the Grass Roots

THE PRECEDING ANALYSES TURN common conceptions of environmental opinion on their head. The usual way of thinking, by scientists and laymen alike, views environmental concern as a stable and widely shared orientation of modern mass publics. The main questions asked by researchers have been what is the scope of the public's environmental worries and which demographic groups are most environmentally conscious. Similarly, the formation of environmental policy has been thought of as a process of representation and compromise, in which leaders arise to speak for environmental interests, these environmental leaders come into conflict with advocates of such other objectives as low taxes and economic growth, and eventually policies are developed that provide moderate levels of environmental protection while allowing other aims to be achieved. Environmentalism is thus viewed as existing prior to and independent of government and top leaders, and the latter, in developing environmental policy, are seen as responding to outside forces.

In reality, the direction of causality appears to run in the opposite direction, from leaders to mass opinion. If the United States and other western industrial democracies have indeed been witnessing an environmental movement, it is a movement whose philosophy is only skin deep. Beneath the scientific arguments and ecological warnings of environmental interest groups are voters with very narrow and mundane concerns. Through their arguments and policy proposals, leaders

```
                    Statement and
                    actions of elites

        The visibility          The principle of
          principle             overriding interests
              |                          |
              |                          |
              |                          |
  Environmental        Environmental              Attitudes
   problems:             concerns:                 toward
  Natural systems        Real and                  policy:
    and built   ------>  anticipated   ------>    Narrow/
  environment            annoyances                 self-
                         in everyday              interested
                            life
```

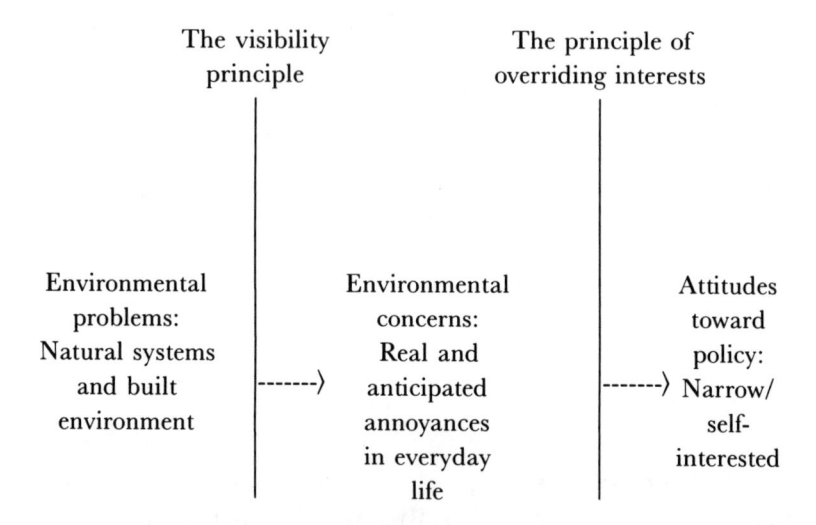

Figure 8.1. The Formation of Environmental Opinion

exert a very powerful influence over the bundling of environmental concerns in mass belief systems and hence also over the lines of coalition and cleavage in the mass public.

The Formation of Environmental Opinion

Elite discourse operates like a magnet or a conceptual scoop, reaching into the mass public and organizing narrow environmental peeves into large, loose, ideological conglomerations. Figure 8-1 is the causal chain we began with in chapter 1, except that its components are described in more detail on the basis of the research presented in subsequent chapters. The easiest way to understand the important role played by elites in the formation of environmental opinion is to consider what environmental attitudes are like before they are, in a sense, activated by the appeals of top leaders.

Environmental problems in Florida and elsewhere include pollution, the destruction of wildlife habitats, resource shortages, overloaded public facilities, and other threats to the natural and social systems. Without assistance from environmental leaders, the public perceives only a few of these factors. It sees those manifestations of urbanization that are visible during workaday routines: traffic, billboards, office buildings near homes, farms being replaced by condominiums. Few people are aware, either directly or through the mass media, of the destruction of wildlife and wildlife habitats, problems with the global ecosystem, or other perturbations of a more distal nature. We have referred to this perceptual screen as a visibility principle.

Because the visibility principle produces what might be called an environmental myopia, people's environmental concerns are concrete and close to home. The bulk of the population is worried about the uglification of the built environment and the inability of the political system to assure that development is orderly and well planned. To be sure, some people are alarmed about the destruction of natural resources and wildlife, but they are a very small segment of the population.

Just as people's environmental concerns are narrow and disjointed, their attitudes toward policies for growth management and environmental protection are based on very limited and mundane objectives. The average person considers how a particular proposal will affect his income, lifestyle, or general situation. In some cases, the implication may be ambiguous, and the individual's position will be uncertain. In other cases where the impacts of a proposed policy are relatively straightforward, people line up according to their overriding interests.

When all of these myopic and self-interested individuals are combined to form a mass public, the result is a kaleidoscope of opinion groups that can be shuffled and recombined in new ways with a simple change of the political arguments, positions, or decisions of top leaders. Everyone applauds environmental protection, but people will quickly become divided if they are confronted by policies with clear winners and losers. Downzoning in an area like the Florida Keys pits land speculators and lot owners against middle-class homeowners worried about overloaded public facilities. A proposed urban growth boundary in a community like Lee County causes the population to sort itself into two groups: environmentalists and those more concerned about economic development. Divisions over policy spring from the policy's anticipated effects on different groups, effects in large part identified and highlighted in elite discourse.

By the same token, the structure and range of environmental coalitions are a consequence of the strategy formulated at the top. When concepts are developed that bridge a variety of concerns, support for environmental protection is likely to be broad based. An example is the whole notion of growth management, a concept that allows for population increases and therefore does not alarm groups interested in economic development, but that also calls for controls on land use and therefore draws in those who are worried about environmental degradation, overloaded public facilities, or undesirable changes in the community's character. Clearly, calls for growth *management* will generate wider support than, say, demands for a growth *cap*.

Moreover, the ways in which environmental issues are conceptualized by top leaders actually influence the public's perception of environmental problems. Where elites place the emphasis on public facilities, as they did in Palm Beach County, the electorate becomes concerned most about traffic, landscaping, billboards, and other aspects of the built environment. Conversely, when leaders focus on containing urban sprawl, as they did in Martin County, the public's attention is directed to zoning decisions involving the urban growth boundary, and environmental concerns center on the equity, consistency and predictability of planning and zoning. The concepts and political strategies of top leaders set the policy agenda, draw the lines of conflict and consensus, and provide the lens through which the electorate perceives and interprets its surroundings. In short, environmentalism is not a set of attitudes; it is a political process bringing attitudes into a conceptual framework.

Implications

These conclusions about environmental opinion have theoretical, methodological and practical implications. The theoretical implication is that different environmental problems, arguments, and policies are likely to mobilize different subgroups of the population. The finding from numerous studies that environmentalism, when measured as a generalized concern, is consistently correlated only with age, education, and political ideology suggests that national and worldwide problems of overpopulation, resource depletion, and environmental degradation are of concern mainly to young, college-educated liberals and radicals who have been sensitized to these issues by their professors. The environmental concerns of other groups stem from localized air and water pollution, gasoline shortages, unsightly urban sprawl, and other calamities that are relatively concrete and immediate. This explains why the ideological and demographic correlates of environmental concern vary so greatly depending on where surveys are conducted and which environmental issues are examined.

The thesis that environmental opinion is shaped by the local environmental and political context suggests that there is a need to shift directions in research. The important focus is not the scope and demographic location of the public's environmental concerns but rather the conditions and political factors that mobilize different types of environmental coalitions. Generally speaking, we have found that conflict at the elite level tends to be mirrored in the mass public. However, much remains to be learned. For example, under what circumstances do people begin to recognize that various environmental problems are connected? What are the limits of the mass public's ability to comprehend ecological processes? What forms of mass communication are most effective in transmitting environmental information? Knowing that environmentalism is a process rather than an attitude is not the same thing as understanding the process itself.

The methodological implication is that researchers should abandon survey designs and statistical techniques that presuppose the existence of a generalized concern for the environment. Survey questions that lump numerous environmental issues together and scales that combine responses to a variety of environmental items are based on faulty premises. They assume that everyone has a concern for the environment that varies only in intensity and in the range of environmental factors to which it applies. In actuality, environmental worries come in small, narrowly focused, self-contained bundles, and concern for any given environmental problem tends to be isolated in a discrete group.

Because environmental opinion is thus fragmented and atomized, the only way to observe it accurately is with methods that allow for diversity among respondents' perspectives. At least three observation methods should be considered. One approach is to employ open-ended questions in random sample surveys. This was the strategy used by Converse and tried with some success in the present study. A second method is "focus groups." These offer a setting where people's views can be explored in detail so that it is possible to understand the basis for their attitudes toward specific issues. Third, analysts may want to conduct interviews with elites. Certainly, there are dangers in relying on elite interviews to draw conclusions about mass opinion, and such interviews should not be used in isolation, but they can be of assistance in interpreting the divisions found in mass surveys of public opinion. Indeed, given the influence elites have on the environmental beliefs of the mass public, it may be impossible to understand the results of opinion surveys without information about the positions of top leaders.

The practical implication of our conclusions is that leaders of the environmental movement are likely to be more successful if they address immediate, localized problems than if they try to enlist support, as Swan (1971) advocates, with abstract arguments about the relation of man to nature. The environmental movement is a coalition of people with very mundane concerns. Hence, in order to expand the movement, leaders need to stress how environmental degradation affects people in the short run and in their everyday lives.

The key is to develop concepts and policies that link the public's discrete, mundane peeves to larger environmental issues. When traffic, water pollution, loss of agricultural lands, and unsightly urban development are all seen as flowing from a single source—uncontrolled growth or poor growth management—a number of separate groups can combine into a unified movement. Rather than formulating concepts from the top down, that is, from complex ecological theories down to problems in everyday life, a better strategy is to work from the bottom up. Very mundane concerns must be linked to more general but still rather localized issues before they can be seen to be part of even more complex and distal processes. The environmental public must learn to crawl before it walks.

The Future of Environmentalism

Those who would draw from these findings pessimistic conclusions about the future of the environmental movement would be mistaken. Admittedly the public's environmental concerns are not as altruistic and global as some social scientists have imagined, and the thesis that environmentalism is a unified national and international political philosophy is definitely incorrect. But this does not mean that the public's environmental concerns will be either short lived or politically inconsequential.

It is precisely because they are locally grounded and personally constructed that environmental concerns will endure and probably mount. Worries about the surrounding environment represent a very salient and yet largely untapped political interest. The political mobilization and targeting of this interest require only that leaders show the general public that their narrow environmental concerns are connected to larger social and economic processes. Once numerous voters recognize that their seemingly individual problems have a common source, collective action beyond the local level will be possible and likely.

The existence of a bedrock of crude environmental concerns among a large segment of the mass public is why very distant ecological problems can arouse widespread alarm so quickly. An oil spill in Alaska will have absolutely no actual effects on the average U.S. citizen in other states, but it nevertheless generates anger and consternation because it is linked in people's minds to environmental problems that are closer to home. If there were no environmental concerns of a local and personal nature, distant catastrophes would spark no more interest than, say, the inflation rate in Brazil or the daily loss of life in Liberia.

The important question is when and how the latent environmentalism of the mass public will be tapped and directed. The main barrier to its political activation is not the narrow focus and parochial orientations of the citizenry, but the cognitive limitations of mass belief systems. Environmental issues are very complex, and it is not clear that people have the technical expertise to understand them in much depth.

Consequently, even if the public's environmental concerns are united into a broad-based social movement, the movement probably will focus on specific issues rather than on the overall political-economic system. Slogans like "save the whales" and "stop pollution" will be on its banners, not "down with capitalism" or "small is beautiful." To have an environmental movement with a philosophical ideology at its grass roots would require a fundamental change in mass belief systems. This does not mean that an environmental movement is impossible, but it does suggest that the movement will remain somewhat locally oriented. Perhaps environmental leaders would achieve more if they tried for less.

Appendix

MOST OF THE DATA contained below were drawn from the 1977 and 1988 *Florida Statistical Abstract* (Gainesville: University of Florida Press). The 1988 *Abstract* was the source for population growth (table 1.20); land area (table 8.03); land in agriculture in 1986 (table 9.45); active driver's licenses (table 13.34); and reported motor vehicle accidents (table 13.49). The 1977 *Abstract* was the source for land area in acres and land area in farms for 1974 (table 9.09). Voting data on the blue belt amendment were taken from *State of Florida General Election Returns, November 8, 1988*, Tabulation of Official Votes by the Florida Department of State, Division of Elections, p. 53.

Almost all of the Florida sites included in this study were counties. The exceptions were the cities of Delray Beach and Sunrise. Delray Beach is in Palm Beach County, which was also the site for two other surveys included in the study. Sunrise is in Broward County. For this reason Broward County is denoted in the tables below as a study site; the Broward data provide an indication of trends and conditions in the city.

A discussion of the indicators and calculations follows each table. The purpose of the discussion is not to analyze the data but rather to describe the measures in the table and point out any of their strengths or weaknesses.

Appendix

Table A-1. Florida Population Growth by County, 1970–87

	1970	1980	1987	Change 1970–87
*Broward	620,100	1,018,300	1,181,000	560,900
Dade	1,267,800	1,625,500	1,802,400	534,600
*Palm Beach	349,000	576,800	789,500	440,500
Hillsborough	490,300	646,900	801,400	311,100
Pinellas	522,300	728,500	828,700	306,400
Orange	344,300	470,900	603,300	259,000
*Lee	105,200	205,300	293,700	188,500
Pasco	76,000	193,700	254,700	178,700
Seminole	87,300	179,822	254,800	167,500
Volusia	169,500	258,800	330,900	161,400
Polk	228,500	321,700	389,100	160,600
Brevard	230,000	273,000	371,700	141,700
Duval	528,900	571,000	664,100	135,200
Sarasota	120,400	202,300	251,300	130,900
Marion	69,000	122,500	174,600	105,600
Collier	38,000	86,000	126,600	88,600
Manatee	97,100	148,400	181,700	84,600
*St. Lucie	50,800	87,200	128,400	77,600
Alachua	104,800	151,400	179,700	74,900
Leon	103,000	148,700	176,500	73,500
Escambia	205,300	233,800	278,400	73,100
Lake	69,300	104,900	137,100	67,800
Clay	32,100	67,100	95,300	63,200
Hernando	17,000	44,500	79,700	62,700
Citrus	19,200	54,700	81,900	62,700
Osceola	25,300	49,300	87,600	62,300
*Martin	28,000	64,000	89,000	61,000
Okaloosa	88,200	109,900	149,000	60,800
Charlotte	27,600	58,500	88,200	60,600
Bay	75,300	97,700	129,700	54,400
*Indian River	36,000	59,900	83,500	47,500
St. Johns	31,000	51,300	75,100	44,100
Highlands	29,500	47,500	63,500	34,000
Santa Rosa	37,700	56,000	66,200	28,500

(continued)

Table A-1—continued

	1970	1980	1987	Change 1970–87
Putnam	36,400	50,500	62,500	26,100
Nassau	20,600	32,900	44,000	23,400
*Monroe	52,600	63,200	74,500	21,900
Okeechobee	11,200	20,300	27,700	16,500
Columbia	25,300	35,400	41,500	16,200
Flagler	4,500	10,900	19,200	14,700
Sumter	14,800	24,300	29,300	14,500
Hendry	11,900	18,600	24,600	12,700
Walton	16,100	21,300	27,500	11,400
Levy	12,800	19,900	23,900	11,100
Suwannee	15,600	22,300	26,200	10,600
DeSoto	13,100	19,000	22,900	9,800
Bradford	14,600	20,000	24,100	9,500
Jackson	34,400	39,200	43,700	9,300
Baker	9,200	15,300	18,400	9,200
Wakulla	6,300	10,900	13,700	7,400
Hardee	14,900	20,400	22,100	7,200
Gadsden	39,200	41,700	46,200	7,000
Holmes	10,700	14,700	16,300	5,600
Taylor	13,600	16,500	18,800	5,200
Dixie	5,500	7,800	9,900	4,400
Washington	11,500	14,500	15,400	3,900
Glades	3,700	6,000	7,400	3,700
Gilchrist	3,600	5,800	7,100	3,500
Jefferson	8,800	10,700	11,900	3,100
Union	8,100	10,200	10,700	2,600
Madison	13,500	14,900	15,900	2,400
Lafayette	2,900	4,000	5,100	2,200
Calhoun	7,600	9,300	9,700	2,100
Gulf	10,100	10,700	12,000	1,900
Hamilton	7,800	8,800	9,400	1,600
Liberty	3,400	4,300	5,000	1,600
Franklin	7,100	7,700	8,500	1,400

*Counties in the study.

The total increase in population rather than the percentage increase is used as an indicator of growth because often the percentage increase is a misleading figure. Very highly populated counties, such as Broward, will show comparatively low rates of growth even though the absolute numbers moving in are very large. In contrast, rural areas that have a low population base to begin with show high rates of growth even when the actual numbers of people moving in are comparatively modest.

Nevertheless, the overall amount of growth experienced in a given area does not necessarily provide a complete picture of the effect that growth is having in the area. Some counties, such as Broward, are already largely urbanized, so even a very high rate and amount of growth may not have a drastic effect on the character of the community. In contrast, a county such as Monroe, which is very fragile environmentally and very narrow geographically, can experience a moderate amount of growth and yet undergo a radical transformation.

Table A-2. Persons per Square Mile by County

	Square miles	Persons per square mile 1987	Persons per square mile 1970	Change in density 1970–87
Pinellas	280	2,959	1,865	1,094
Seminole	298	855	292	563
*Broward	1,211	975	512	463
Hillsborough	1,053	761	465	296
Orange	910	662	378	284
Dade	1,955	921	648	273
Pasco	738	345	102	243
*Lee	803	365	131	234
Sarasota	573	438	210	228
*Palm Beach	1,993	396	175	221
Duval	776	855	681	174
Volusia	1,113	297	152	145
Brevard	995	373	231	142

(*continued*)

Table A-2—continued

	Square miles	Persons per square mile 1987	Persons per square mile 1970	Change in density 1970–87
*St. Lucie	581	220	87	133
Hernando	477	167	35	132
Manatee	747	243	129	114
Escambia	661	421	310	111
*Martin	555	160	50	110
Leon	676	261	152	109
Clay	592	160	54	106
Citrus	629	130	30	100
*Indian River	497	168	72	96
Polk	1,823	213	125	88
Charlotte	690	127	40	87
Alachua	902	199	116	83
Bay	758	171	99	72
St. Johns	617	121	50	71
Lake	954	143	72	71
Marion	1,610	108	42	66
Okaloosa	936	159	94	65
Osceola	1,350	64	18	46
Collier	1,994	63	19	44
Nassau	649	67	31	36
Putnam	733	85	49	36
Highlands	1,029	61	28	33
Bradford	293	82	49	33
Flagler	491	39	9	30
Santa Rosa	1,024	64	36	28
Sumter	561	52	26	26
*Monroe	1,034	72	50	22
Okeechobee	771	35	14	21
Columbia	797	52	31	21
DeSoto	636	36	20	16
Baker	585	31	15	16
Suwannee	690	37	22	15

(continued)

Table A-2—*continued*

	Square miles	Persons per square mile 1987	Persons per square mile 1970	Change in density 1970–87
Gadsden	518	89	75	14
Holmes	488	33	21	12
Wakulla	601	22	10	12
Union	246	43	32	11
Hardee	637	34	23	11
Hendry	1,163	21	10	11
Jackson	942	46	36	10
Gilchrist	354	20	10	10
Levy	1,100	21	11	10
Walton	1,066	25	15	10
Washington	590	26	19	7
Dixie	701	14	7	7
Taylor	1,058	17	12	5
Glades	763	9	4	5
Jefferson	609	19	14	5
Calhoun	568	17	13	4
Lafayette	545	9	5	4
Madison	710	22	19	3
Hamilton	517	18	15	3
Gulf	559	21	18	3
Franklin	545	15	13	2
Liberty	837	5	4	1

*Counties in the study.

Persons per square mile is calculated by dividing the population figures from table A-1 by the square mile figures in table A-2. The change in density is calculated by subtracting the persons per square mile in 1970 from the persons per square mile in 1987.

The density or persons per square mile is a good measure of urbanization, but it has some drawbacks. The biggest weakness is that the total square miles listed in table A-2 gives no indication of how much of the land included in the county is actually developable. For example, about two-thirds of Broward County's 1,211 square miles are made up of Everglades, which will never be open to urbanization. Similarly, Palm Beach County has a very large agriculture area that generally is not part of the urbanizing land in the county. Hence the density shown for these and similar counties is understated.

Table A-3. Acreage in Agriculture by County, 1974–86

	Acreage in agriculture 1974	1986	Total acreage	% Acreage in agriculture 1986	% Change 1974–86
*Broward	51,247	36,731	779,968	4	−28
Pasco	315,736	260,500	474,624	54	−17
Glades	537,544	443,500	481,920	92	−17
Osceola	869,358	730,000	840,320	86	−16
Hernando	79,010	75,000	309,952	24	−5
Hendry	744,484	734,484	759,680	96	−1
Manatee	373,449	382,000	473,088	80	2
Sarasota	223,061	235,000	375,872	62	5
Polk	736,107	791,800	1,189,120	66	7
Hardee	297,934	326,302	402,688	81	9
*St. Lucie	324,479	354,673	373,440	94	9
Dade	80,896	89,908	1,306,816	6	11
Marion	519,646	585,000	1,123,680	52	12
Okeechobee	380,260	465,500	497,280	93	22
*Palm Beach	515,927	635,000	1,294,720	49	23
*Indian River	187,246	236,664	324,096	73	26
DeSoto	270,330	354,000	414,528	85	30
Brevard	251,112	336,000	647,040	51	33
Highlands	437,958	596,708	638,080	93	36
Hillsborough	362,487	527,546	664,192	79	45
Charlotte	176,446	259,148	449,920	57	46
*Martin	214,841	319,000	355,840	89	48
Orange	224,723	344,745	582,400	59	53
Lake	316,351	515,245	614,784	83	62

(*continued*)

Table A-3—*continued*

	Acreage in agriculture 1974	Acreage in agriculture 1986	Total acreage	% Acreage in agriculture 1986	% Change 1974–86
Alachua	276,891	462,550	586,048	78	67
Sumter	189,281	338,426	355,264	95	78
Seminole	63,365	116,000	195,136	59	83
Suwannee	228,179	427,000	438,912	97	87
Madison	167,860	324,700	449,856	72	93
Clay	142,321	278,000	379,520	73	95
Jackson	285,956	572,212	598,528	95	100
Collier	286,754	576,448	1,283,968	44	101
Gadsden	107,472	228,243	327,872	69	112
Gilchrist	97,360	210,000	221,632	94	115
Leon	139,615	307,000	428,928	71	119
Putnam	178,402	416,568	498,368	83	133
Okaloosa	86,066	203,630	604,352	33	136
Union	62,905	150,919	154,240	97	139
Jefferson	142,053	346,073	387,328	89	143
Holmes	123,332	305,560	308,352	99	147
Citrus	103,339	263,075	358,208	73	154
Levy	267,569	684,000	692,800	98	155
*Lee	132,504	383,325	502,400	76	189
Columbia	140,218	410,523	501,824	81	192
Volusia	184,604	549,000	679,616	80	197
Hamilton	101,734	319,763	329,088	97	214
Duval	91,332	307,000	490,048	62	236
Flagler	86,310	290,040	311,872	92	236
Bradford	48,583	168,000	187,968	89	245
Pinellas	18,633	64,737	169,408	38	247
Escambia	91,563	332,994	425,600	78	263
Dixie	104,129	398,000	443,136	89	282
Washington	86,631	355,995	374,592	95	310
Lafayette	80,086	345,500	351,168	98	331
Walton	117,130	513,400	673,600	76	338
Santa Rosa	94,031	454,563	660,352	68	383

(*continued*)

Table A-3—*continued*

	Acreage in agriculture 1974	Acreage in agriculture 1986	Total acreage	% Acreage in agriculture 1986	% Change 1974–86
Taylor	116,165	573,280	672,384	85	393
Nassau	61,083	350,134	416,000	84	473
Gulf	60,126	350,000	361,408	96	482
Calhoun	57,921	355,808	358,912	99	514
Baker	42,787	285,320	374,144	76	566
St. Johns	42,364	324,400	387,008	83	665
Wakulla	11,908	160,472	384,384	41	1247
Liberty	17,259	268,000	536,704	49	1452
Bay	19,853	410,490	478,336	85	1967
*Monroe			Not Available		
Franklin			Not Available		

*Counties in the study.

The percentage of land in agriculture is another measure of urbanization, but it has weaknesses similar to the density measure discussed earlier. The main problem is that the acreage in agriculture does not necessarily cover all of the open or undeveloped land in the county. Much land will be totally undeveloped, such as pasture lands, wetlands, lakes, and forest land. Consequently, even though a given county may be urbanizing rapidly, it need not experience a reduction in the amount of land in agriculture, and it may even experience an increase. This is clear in table A-3. Many of the counties in Florida experienced an increase in the overall acreage in agriculture between 1974 and 1986. During this time, much land that had been in pastures or wetlands was drained for framing. Still, table A-3 does give an indication of the spread of urban development in Florida's counties. It also shows that as urbanization proceeds, agriculture is pushed off of existing farms and into areas that are often environmentally special or ecologically sensitive.

Table A-4. Accident Rates by County, 1986

	Active driver's licenses	Reported accidents	Accidents per 1,000 licenses
Leon	135,388	5,340	39
*Monroe	70,398	2,284	32
Hillsborough	662,688	20,559	31
Hamilton	6,755	199	29
Orange	525,064	15,682	29
Glades	3,579	104	29
Gadsden	25,193	713	28
Dade	1,420,722	39,976	28
Taylor	13,183	374	28
Duval	522,333	14,115	27
Bradford	14,489	394	27
DeSoto	16,537	422	25
Osceola	73,266	1,854	25
Polk	303,377	7,602	25
*Broward	1,050,996	25,844	24
Walton	18,002	441	24
Wakulla	7,197	174	24
Collier	115,373	2,688	23
Escambia	216,415	5,119	23
Columbia	30,381	729	23
Volusia	294,855	6,822	23
Jefferson	7,552	176	23
Jackson	30,619	714	23
*St. Lucie	103,045	2,429	23
Manatee	160,805	3,704	23
*Lee	261,343	6,030	23
*Martin	83,146	1,860	22
Sumter	23,242	517	22
Bay	106,847	2,429	22
Putnam	45,088	1,011	22
St. Johns	66,502	1,524	22
Alachua	141,390	3,170	22
Nassau	33,393	722	21
Marion	152,184	3,229	21

(*continued*)

Table A-4—*continued*

	Active driver's licenses	Reported accidents	Accidents per 1,000 licenses
Okeechobee	23,591	518	21
*Palm Beach	716,506	15,397	21
Hendry	19,113	401	20
Hardee	15,609	319	20
Madison	11,260	216	19
Highlands	51,726	991	19
Brevard	320,950	6,124	19
Seminole	198,517	3,787	19
Dixie	6,527	128	19
Liberty	3,413	64	18
Calhoun	6,763	128	18
*Indian River	74,259	1,350	18
Santa Rosa	58,935	1,080	18
Suwannee	19,773	339	17
Lake	117,511	2,059	17
Pinellas	733,152	12,914	17
Washington	12,636	218	17
Union	5,528	97	17
Charlotte	76,466	1,360	17
Baker	10,995	181	16
Flagler	18,546	307	16
Citrus	66,778	1,069	16
Holmes	10,639	177	16
Sarasota	252,363	4,203	16
Lafayette	2,596	44	16
Pasco	208,063	3,247	15
Okaloosa	123,078	1,952	15
Franklin	6,782	104	15
Hernando	74,799	1,087	14
Clay	79,152	1,185	14
Levy	19,234	254	13
Gilchrist	5,821	71	12
Gulf	9,017	91	10

*Counties in the study.

The accidents per 1,000 licenses is intended to get at one of the most vexing aspects of urban growth: traffic and its associated hazards. However, this measure does not directly tap the thing that seems to bother motorists most, that is, the amount of time wasted sitting at lights and in traffic jams. Also, because the measure is based on a yearlong period, it does not take into account the higher levels of traffic congestion and the larger number of accidents that occur in certain areas of Florida during the tourist season. For example, Dade, Broward, Palm Beach, and Monroe counties would all have very high accident rates if the measure extrapolated from the experience in these counties during the November to March tourist influx. Many retirees, who sometimes have deficiencies as drivers, come to Florida only during the winter months. Thus in south Florida the roads are especially crowded and are loaded with very hazardous drivers during a small part of the year, and at these times the accident rate would be very high.

Table A-5. Florida Population Growth and Vote on the Blue Belt Amendment by County

	1970–87 Growth	Blue Belt For	Blue Belt Against	% For
Orange	259,000	125,031	34,555	78
Sarasota	130,900	86,504	23,395	78
Seminole	167,500	57,491	16,609	77
Flagler	14,700	7,389	2,089	77
Volusia	161,400	71,339	20,669	77
Lake	67,800	31,758	10,382	75
Brevard	141,700	100,209	35,004	74
*Broward	560,900	276,565	96,899	74
Leon	73,500	41,077	15,284	72
*Palm Beach	440,500	195,194	82,327	70
Sumter	14,500	5,856	2,501	70
Osceola	62,300	18,916	7,972	70
Manatee	84,600	49,670	21,106	70
Marion	105,600	38,493	16,974	69
Hillsborough	311,100	142,667	65,189	68

(*continued*)

Table A-5—*continued*

	1970–87 Growth	Blue Belt For	Blue Belt Against	% For
Gadsden	7,000	5,696	2,780	67
*St. Lucie	77,600	28,409	14,603	66
Alachua	74,900	33,632	16,713	66
Escambia	73,100	45,594	23,949	65
Dade	534,600	2,508,311	29,614	65
Collier	88,600	27,958	15,054	65
*Martin	61,000	22,122	11,707	65
Highlands	34,000	14,589	8,036	64
*Indian River	47,500	19,083	11,137	63
DeSoto	9,800	3,577	2,076	63
Hendry	12,700	3,086	1,808	63
Glades	3,700	1,380	822	62
Jefferson	3,100	2,297	1,382	62
*Monroe	21,900	14,403	8,551	62
Pinellas	306,400	1,938,791	23,239	61
Okaloosa	60,800	24,716	15,547	61
*Lee	188,500	69,539	44,040	61
Santa Rosa	28,500	14,476	9,287	60
Charlotte	60,600	21,459	14,002	60
Pasco	178,700	60,340	39,334	60
Hernando	62,700	21,619	14,353	60
Hardee	7,200	2,147	1,461	59
Okeechobee	16,500	3,222	2,183	59
Duval	135,200	101,736	69,940	59
Madison	2,400	2,356	1,696	58
Clay	63,200	17,308	12,509	58
Dixie	4,400	1,772	1,282	58
Levy	11,100	3,635	2,631	58
Gilchrist	3,500	1,614	1,149	58
St. Johns	44,100	13,586	10,156	57
Taylor	5,200	2,520	1,875	57
Walton	11,400	4,571	3,569	56
Bay	54,400	19,087	14,742	56
Polk	160,600	57,257	44,386	56

(*continued*)

Table A-5—*continued*

	1970–87 Growth	Blue Belt For	Blue Belt Against	% For
Wakulla	7,400	2,344	1,855	55
Nassau	23,400	5,996	4,860	55
Citrus	62,700	17,111	14,011	54
Jackson	9,300	5,138	4,328	54
Putnam	26,100	9,930	8,574	53
Hamilton	1,600	1,115	1,017	52
Franklin	1,400	1,274	1,166	52
Washington	3,900	2,409	2,311	51
Suwannee	10,600	3,430	3,184	51
Bradford	9,500	2,886	2,782	50
Liberty	1,600	727	741	49
Union	2,600	926	961	49
Columbia	16,200	5,486	5,597	49
Calhoun	2,100	1,271	1,395	47
Baker	9,200	1,935	2,345	45
Holmes	5,600	1,848	2,431	43
Lafayette	2,200	731	942	43
Gulf	1,900	1,571	2,235	41

*Counties in the study.

The blue belt amendment was on the statewide ballot in November 1988. It authorized a preferential assessment for ad valorem taxes on land that is undeveloped and provides open space so that rainfall recharges the underground aquifers holding much of Florida's water supply. The blue belt amendment is the only statewide environmental issue that allows a county-to-county comparison in Florida during the 1980s. Generally, support for the amendment indicates a pro-environmental stance.

Notes

Chapter 1
1. This argument is presented in deHaven-Smith (1989).

Chapter 2
1. The survey was conducted by the Social Science Research Laboratory at Florida Atlantic University. A proportionate, stratified, random sample of residential phone numbers across the nation was provided by Survey Sampling, Inc. To ensure that unlisted phone numbers were included in the sample, the last two digits of the phone numbers selected were replaced by numbers generated randomly by computer. Once contact was made, individuals were selected for the interview choosing alternately the youngest male eighteen or over, the youngest female eighteen or over, the oldest male, or the oldest female. Once respondents were successfully screened, the response rate for completion of the interviews was 65 percent. The sample size was 636.

2. The exact wording of these questions was: *national level*—"What do you think is the most important problem facing this country today?"; *state level*—"Now, I'd like to talk about your state. What do you think is the most important problem facing your state?"; *local level*—"Next, I'd like to ask you about your community, city, or town. What do you think is the biggest problem facing your community?"

3. The exact wording of the questions referenced in table 1-2 was: *national level*—"How worried are you about . . . improving roads and highways?, . . . shortages of oil, gasoline, coal, natural gas, electricity, or other fuels?, . . . the disposal of hazardous chemical wastes?, . . . the presence of toxic chemicals such as pesticides

or PCBs in the environment?, . . . reducing air pollution?, . . . protecting wildlife and endangered species?"; *state level*—"How worried are you about population growth in your state?, How about . . . the types of people moving into your state?, . . . roads and highways?, . . . preservation of scenic areas, such as beaches and rivers?, . . . protection of agricultural areas?, . . . water and air pollution?, . . . protection of wildlife?"; *local level*—"How worried are you about rapid growth in your community?, How about . . . the types of people moving into your area? . . . traffic congestion?, . . . quality of development, including density and height of buildings?, . . . pollution of scenic areas, such as parks and beaches?, . . . local water quality?"

Chapter 3

1. Following are the population figures for Florida between 1950 and 1980.

Year	Population	Change from previous decade
1950	2,771,305	873,891
1960	4,951,560	2,180,255
1970	6,791,418	1,839,858
1980	9,746,324	2,954,906

2. Florida's population increased from 6,791,418 in 1970 to 9,746,324 in 1980, an increase of almost three million people. Of this increase, 33 percent occurred in what is referred to here as the southern region, 57 percent in the central region, and 10 percent in the northern region (*Florida Statistical Abstract*, pp. 36–37). The regions are depicted in figure 3-1.

3. *River of Grass* is the title of Marjory Stoneman Douglas's book on the Everglades.

4. The state's backlog in public facilities is estimated by some sources to be in the neighborhood of $50 billion.

5. State guidelines and standards identify twelve types of activity of a size presumed to be of regional impact. These include large residential developments, regional shopping centers, office parks, phosphate mining projects, schools, airports, amusement parks, port facilities, electrical transmission lines, petroleum storage facilities, and hospitals.

6. The survey was funded by the Florida Atlantic University/Florida International University Joint Center for Environmental and Urban Problems. It was conducted between 17 October and 19 December 1984.

7. The sample included 327 respondents from the northern region, 290 from the central region, and 273 from the southern region. The sample of phone numbers was purchased from Survey Sampling, Inc. Respondents were eighteen years old or older. A three-step procedure was used to construct the sample. First, a proportionate, stratified, random sample of listed residential phone numbers was drawn on the

basis of the number of residential listings per Central Office Code (telephone prefix) in each county, with the number of telephone numbers drawn from each county based on the county's population as a proportion of the region. Second, to ensure that unlisted phone numbers were included in the sample, the last two digits of the phone numbers selected in the first step were replaced by numbers generated randomly by a computer. Third, following the approach developed by Hagen and Collier (1982), selective sampling within households was employed to ensure adequate representation of sexes and ages. A total of 1,253 working residential phone numbers were selected, and, from these, 890 interviews were completed. Thus the response rate was 71 percent.

8. The wording of the questions is presented below. The names of the question, as referred to in table 3-1, appear in parentheses.

Next I'm going to read you a list of things that some people think the state government here in Florida should do, and that some people think that the state should not do. I want you to tell me how you personally feel. Do you think the state government should or should not:

(Prevent pollution 1) Have stronger laws to prevent pollution of the air and water. . . .

Next I would like for you to tell me whether you personally agree or disagree with some things that people sometimes tell us:

(Protect wildlife) Florida needs stronger laws to protect its fish and wildlife from land development on the state's woodlands and beaches.

(Conserve water) Florida has a plentiful supply of water and doesn't need water conservation regulation.

(Anti-economic development) We need economic growth and development in Florida even if it endangers the natural environment.

(Prevent pollution 2) Florida needs stronger laws to prevent pollution of its air and water.

(Strengthen zoning) Generally speaking, would you favor relaxing land use regulations to permit more land development, strengthening land use regulations to reduce development or improve its quality, or leaving land use regulations pretty much as they are now?

Note that responses to all questions were coded so that they increased in magnitude with a pro-environmental policy.

9. In contrast to the usual approach of correlating environmental attitudes with demographic variables—an approach that provides observations of the relationship between different subgroups on the same issue or dimension—this method provides observations of the relationships between attitudes within different subgroups.

Chapter 4

1. Funding for the survey was provided by the Treasure Coast Regional Planning Council. The sample of phone numbers was purchased from Survey Sampling, Inc.

A three-step sampling procedure was used. First, a proportionate, stratified, random sample of residential telephone numbers was drawn on the basis of the number of residential listings per Central Office Code (telephone prefix) in each county. Second, the last two digits of the phone numbers selected in the first step were replaced by numbers generated randomly by a computer. Third, following the approach developed by Hagan and Collier (1982), random sampling of individuals within households was also employed prior to each interview once telephone contact was made. Respondents were eighteen years or older. The sample was constructed so that each county had at least eighty interviews. The survey was run between 31 May and 15 June 1986. This chapter is drawn largely from deHaven-Smith (1988a).

2. The exact wording for the initial question was: "In your view, should land use regulation, such as zoning and planning, be strengthened, relaxed, or left as it is?" The follow-up question was, "All right. Could you tell us why it is that you want land use regulation strengthened/relaxed/left as it is?"

3. The frequency distribution from responses to the land use regulation question is not shown, but it can be calculated from the column N's. In total, 57 percent of the sample favored strengthening land use regulation, 35.7 percent wanted regulation left as it is, and 6.0 percent advocated relaxation.

4. Each of the questions was designed to tap the public's views on an issue relevant to the Treasure Coast Regional Planning Council's efforts to develop a Comprehensive Regional Policy Plan as mandated under Florida's State and Regional Planning Act of 1984. The questions were as follows:

> (Density): Just for the sake of this next question, let's say that taxes go up when development is spread out to prevent crowding, and that taxes go down when development is packed into small areas. Assuming that this is true, which type of future development should the Treasure Coast region encourage? [options were read]: (1) spread-out development, even though taxes go up; (2) tight, citylike development so that taxes will go down; (3) not sure.
>
> (Environmental risk): Which of the following statements comes closest to your own opinion: (1) if there is any possibility that a new subdivision or office complex will harm the natural environment, then the government should not allow it to be built; (2) government should be concerned about the natural environment, but not so concerned that it is unwilling to take chances when allowing a new subdivision or office complex to be built; (3) government should be concerned less with the environment than with making sure that there are plenty of houses and jobs.
>
> (Infrastructure): Which of the following statements comes closest to your own opinion: (1) if the roads are overcrowded, government should not allow any new offices and houses to be built; (2) if the roads are overcrowded, government should make sure that the construction of new houses and offices does not make the traffic any worse; (3) even if the roads become more

crowded, government should still allow new offices and houses to be built; (4) not sure.

(Agland incentives): In your view, should farmers be given more tax breaks or other incentives to keep their land in agriculture? (1) yes (2) no (3) not sure.

5. Responses of "not sure" were excluded.

Chapter 5

1. Funding for the survey was provided by the Sunrise City Council. The survey questions were designed in consultation with the Sunrise Citizens Advisory Board. The survey was run between 14 July and 3 August 1986. Telephone interviews were conducted with 455 residents, eighteen years old or older, whose phone numbers were selected at random. A three-step sampling procedure was used. First, a proportionate, stratified, random sample of residential telephone numbers was drawn on the basis of residential listings per Central Office Code (telephone prefix) in the city. Second, the last two digits of the phone numbers selected in the first step were replaced by numbers generated randomly by a computer. Third, random sampling of individuals within households was also employed prior to each interview once telephone contact was made.

2. The exact wording of the questions was:

Next, I would like to read you a list of issues that some people have told us are big problems in Sunrise and others have said we should not worry about. I would like to know whether you personally think they are big problems or not.

What about the condition of the roads—not the traffic, but potholes and things like that. Do you personally think the condition of the roads in Sunrise is a big problem, or is it not a big problem?

What about traffic? Do you personally think that traffic in Sunrise is a big problem?

OK, one more. What about crime? Do you personally think that crime is a big problem in Sunrise, or is it not a big problem?

3. The wording was: "In your view, what is the biggest problem that Sunrise has? . . . OK, what do you personally think will be the most serious problem Sunrise will have five years from now?"

4. The wording was:" First, we'd like to hear your views about city services and taxes. Thinking specifically about taxes and services in Sunrise, which of the following statements comes closest to your own opinion: (1) city taxes and services should be increased; (2) city taxes and services should be reduced; (3) city taxes and services should be left about as they are now."

5. The exact wording of the questions was:

OK, next I am going to read you a list of services and facilities provided by the city government in Sunrise, and for each one I would like for you to tell me whether you personally want these services or facilities increased, reduced, or left about as they are now.

Let's begin with the city's bus system, particularly with regard to the number of different routes that the Sunrise bus system offers and the time interval between buses. Would you like to see the city's bus services increased, reduced, or left about as they stand now?

OK, let's move on now to recreational services. Let's start with facilities for sports and recreation like baseball, soccer, shuffleboard, swimming, and so on. Would you like to see the number of sports facilities increased in your neighborhood, reduced, or left about as it is now?

All right, set aside for the moment the question about sports facilities and think about parks. By parks, we mean open areas that would have picnic tables, barbecue grills, nature trails, and playgrounds for children. Would you like to see the number of parks increased, reduced, or left about as it is now?

All right, what about the city's police services? Would you want police services increased, reduced, or left about as they are now?

OK, what about the city's ambulance and emergency medical services? Would you like to see these services increased, reduced, or left about as they are now?

OK, just one more. What about social services for senior citizens, the poor, and the handicapped? These services include nursing care, home meals programs, and the like. Would you want such services increased, reduced, or left about as they are now?

6. Partial funding for the survey was provided as a public service by the Florida Atlantic University/Florida International University Joint Center for Environmental and Urban Problems. The survey was run between 18 September and 7 October 1984. Computer-assisted telephone interviews were conducted with 336 residents whose phone numbers were selected at random.

A three-step sampling procedure was used. First, a proportionate, stratified, random sample of residential telephone numbers was drawn on the basis of the number of residential listings per Central Office Code (Telephone prefix) in the county. Second, the last two digits of the phone numbers selected in the first step were replaced by numbers generated randomly by a computer. Third, following the approach developed by Hagen and Collier (1982), random sampling of individuals within households was also employed prior to each interview once telephone contact was made.

7. The exact question wording was, "In your view, is the quality of the natural environment in Lee County getting better, getting worse, or not changing?"

8. The wording was: "Do you think that the Lee County government should try to attract business and industry into the area, or do you think it should let the economy develop on its own? How much more in taxes each year would you be willing to pay to have the Lee County government try to attract business and industry into the area?"

9. The exact question wording was:

> Now I am going to read you a list of governments, and I want you to evaluate the job that each one has been doing in regulating development and construction in Lee County. Let's start with the federal government. Has it been regulating development too much, not enough, or about the right amount?
>
> All right, what about the Lee County government? Has it been regulating development too much, not enough, or about the right amount?
>
> How about the city government of Ft. Myers? Has it been regulating development too much, not enough or about the right amount?
>
> What about the state government? Has it been regulating development too much, not enough, or about the right amount?

10. Funding was provided by the city council. The survey was run between 26 June and 22 July 1985. Computer-assisted telephone interviews were conducted with 435 residents whose phone numbers were selected at random. A three-step sampling procedure was used. First, a proportionate, stratified, random sample of residential telephone numbers was drawn on the basis of the number of residential listings per Central Office Code (telephone prefix) in the city. Second, the last two digits of the phone numbers selected in the first step were replaced by numbers generated randomly by a computer. Third, random sampling of individuals within households was also employed prior to each interview once telephone contact was made.

11. The exact wording of the question was, "In your view, is the 'quality of life' in Delray Beach getting better, getting worse, or not changing?"

12. The exact wording of the questions was:

> I would like to read you a list of issues that some people have told us are big problems in Delray Beach and others have said we should not worry about. I would like to know whether you personally think they are big problems or not.
>
> Let's begin with traffic. Do you think that the traffic in Delray Beach is a big problem, or that it's not a big problem?
>
> OK, what about crime? In your view, is crime a big problem in Delray Beach, or is it not a big problem?
>
> What about the cost of housing in Delray Beach? Do you think that this is a big problem, or is it not a big problem?

What about the run-down condition of some areas of the city? In your view is this a big problem, or is it not a big problem?

How about the way buildings for businesses are sometimes located in neighborhoods where people live? Do you think that this is a big problem in Delray Beach, or is it not a big problem?

OK, one more. What about the loss of open areas of land around the city? Do you think the loss of open areas is a big problem, or is it not a big problem?

13. The exact wording of the question was: "Next, we would like to know what you think about allowing office buildings to be constructed in Delray Beach. Office buildings can be a good source of tax revenue for Delray Beach, but they can also lead to traffic on the roads. In your view, should the city allow more office buildings to be built?"

14. The exact wording of the question was: "What if the office building were in or near the neighborhood where you live? Would you be willing to acept an office building in or near your neighborhood regardless of the conditions, only under certain conditions, or not at all?"

15. The exact wording of the question was: "As it stands, the city of Delray Beach does not allow new buildings to be more than four stories high. With regard to this policy, which of the following statements comes closest to your view: (1) buildings taller than four stories should be allowed regardless of the conditions; (2) buildings taller than four stories should be allowed if more open space around the buildings is provided; (3) buildings taller than four stories should not be allowed under any circumstances; (4) don't know, not sure."

Chapter 6

1. This assumption is so pervasive that it is usually stated as an established fact rather than as a hypothesis. For example, Seley says: "Controversies over public facilities often center around concerns with changes in the quality of life. Property values, crime, increased traffic, and psychological harm typically are cited, along with public health." Popper offers a similarly economistic analysis: "At the heart of every LULU lie large negative externalities. A LULU may be noisy (airports), dangerous (hazardous waste facilities), ugly (power plants), smelly (many factories), or polluting (all of the above). It may offend its neighbors because of such intrinsic features as its technology or occupants—or it may offend because of its consequences—increased traffic, industrial by-products, or the problems its mismanagement could create." The same perspective can also be found in discussions of unpopular types of private development. Here is how O'Hare, Bacow, and Sanderson described the opponents of unwanted private development: "Although some opponents live in host communities, they just as often come from neighboring towns. These neighbors expect to receive nothing but public and private costs from a nearby development—more population, more traffic, more pollution, more noise."

See Seley (1983, p. 7); Popper (1987, p. 2); O'Hare, Bacow, and Sanderson (1983, p. 7).

2. This section is drawn largely from deHaven-Smith (1985b). The survey was funded by grants from the Palm Beach County Board of Commissioners and the Chastain Foundation. It was conducted between 12 March and 25 March 1984. A proportionate stratified sample of Central Office Codes (telephone prefixes) was drawn on the basis of the number of residential listings per Central Office Code in the county. Four digits were assigned randomly to the Central Office Codes to complete the telephone numbers in the sample. Following the approach developed by Hagen and Collier (1982), selective sampling within households was employed to ensure adequate representation of sexes and ages.

3. The question was: "An amendment that would limit the revenues of all Florida governments, sometimes known as Proposition 1, will be on the November 1984 Florida ballot. If the election were held today, would you vote for or against this amendment?"

4. Crosstabulations of demographic variables and positions on Amendment 1 are presented in deHaven-Smith (1984a, p. 10).

5. The question for those who planned to vote for or against the amendment was, "What is it about Proposition 1 that leads you to plan to vote for (against) it?" For those who were undecided, the question was, "What information about Proposition 1 would most influence your decision about how to vote?"

6. The question was: "Next I would like to hear your ideas about cutting government budgets. Suppose that Florida governments suddenly had their budgets reduced very much. In response to the budget reduction, some services might be cut back, some might be increased, some might be left unchanged, some might be arranged so that they are paid for by fees from those getting the services, and some might be eliminated and left for the private sector to provide. I will read through a list of services, and first I would like for you to tell me what you yourself would want Florida's governments to do. Then I will read the list of services again and ask you to tell me what you would expect Florida's governments to do. Let's begin with what you yourself would want."

The alternatives were presented again after each service was described. Responses for both preferences and expectations were coded as (1) increase; (2) leave as is; (3) reduce; (4) finance by user-charges; and (5) eliminate or privatize. The services were described as follows: education; aid to the poor; construction and maintenance of roads and highways; parks, libraries, and recreational services; utilities, such as water supply and garbage pickup; government employment for record keeping and management.

7. Following Blalock's (1979, pp. 286–87) recommendation, preferences and expectations were recoded in the calculation of Chi square and Gamma because of the large number of small cells. The reduce, fee-basis, and privatization responses were collapsed into one category.

8. A three-step sampling procedure was used for the countywide sample. First, a proportionate, stratified, random sample of residential telephone numbers was drawn on the basis of the number of residential listings per Central Office Code (telephone prefix) in the county. Second, to ensure that unlisted phone numbers were included in the sample, the last two digits of the phone numbers selected in the first step were replaced by numbers generated randomly by a computer. Third, random sampling of individuals within households was also employed prior to each interview once telephone contact was made. A similar sampling frame was used for the five catchment areas, except that the last two digits of the phone numbers were not randomized. Random digit dialing was precluded in the catchment areas because the samples had to be pulled by zip codes. The samples of telephone numbers were purchased from Survey Sampling, Inc.

9. The exact wording of the question was: "(1) The county recognizes a need to upgrade the existing road system. For the sake of the next questions, I would like for you to assume that the county is faced with a difficult decision about a particular road project. Let's say that if the county builds this road, a neighborhood near it won't be as nice to live in. The road will cause an increase in traffic and noise, a possible breach in security, safety, and privacy, as well as a change in the ambience of the community. But if the county does not build the road, residents from all around will have a hard time getting to work, school, and shopping centers. In your view, should the county government build the new road, or should it not?

(2) Recognizing that the county is running out of space for trash in existing trashfills, decisions will have to be made concerning where to locate future trashfills. If it builds the landfill, neighborhoods nearby might be affected. These neighborhoods may experience a loss of property value, increased traffic, or a breach of privacy and security. But if it does not build the landfill, all county residents will have to pay more to get rid of their trash. In your view, should the county government build the trashfill, or should it not?"

10. The exact wording of the question was : "(1) The county has purchased land for a north county airport at Beeline Highway and PGA Boulevard. This site is within three miles of existing residential neighborhoods. The purpose of the airport is to remove some of the small plane traffic from Palm Beach International Airport. Do you personally think the county government should develop the new north county airport for small aircraft, or do you think it should not develop the new airport?

(2) There are proposals to put additional road connections in between Broward and Palm Beach Counties. Some people say that we should have more roads running from north to south to connect the two counties so that it would be easier to get back and forth. Other people say that connecting roads would just allow Broward Couty traffic to spill over into southern Palm Beach County. Do you personally think that more road connections between the two counties should be built, or do you think they should not be built?

(3) There is a proposal to extend the Sawgrass Expressway through Palm Beach County. Initially, this proposal calls for the Sawgrass Expressway to be extended north along the conservation area in the western part of the county and temporarily end at West Atlantic Boulevard in Delray Beach. In the distant future the Sawgrass Expressway is proposed to extend north through Palm Beach County while improving the financial viability of the expressway. Should the expressway be built, or should it not be built?"

11. A brief description of the project(s) was read to the respondent, and then the question was asked about whether the county should proceed. The exact wording of the questions was as follows: "(1) South County: Do you personally think that a turnpike overpass should be constructed for Southwest Eighteenth Street, or should it not be constructed? (2) Lake Ida: In your view, should Lake Ida Road be extended to Jog Road, or should it not be extended? (3) Woolbright Road: In your view, should Woolbright Road be extended to Jog Road, or should it not be extended? (4) North County: Do you personally think Center Street should be widened, or do you think it should not be widened? (5) Do you personally think Prosperity Farms Road should be widened, or do you think it should not be widened? (6) Do you personally think the county government should continue to plan for Hood Road or not? (7) West Palm Beach: Do you personally think that an east-west expressway should be built, or do you think that it should not be built?"

12. The exact wording of the question was, "What do you personally think is the most serious problem in Palm Beach County?"

Chapter 7

1. The 1985 public opinion survey and the lot owner survey were funded by Florida's Department of Community Affairs. The 1984 and 1986 surveys were paid for by the Florida Atlantic University/Florida International University Joint Center for Environmental and Urban Problems. The three surveys of public opinion had approximately the same number of respondents and were conducted almost exactly one year apart. The first survey included 408 interviews and was run between 22 August and 1 September 1984. The second survey had a sample of 399 and was implemented between 15 November and 2 December 1985. The third survey had 408 respondents and was conducted between 21 November and 12 December 1986. The lot owner survey was conducted between 3 December and 22 December 1985. The sample included 114 lot owners. All four of the surveys were conducted over the telephone. A two-step sampling procedure was used to select the telephone numbers in the samples. First, a proportionate, stratified, random sample of residential telephone numbers was drawn on the basis of the number of residential listings per Central Office Code (telephone prefix) in the county. Second, to ensure that unlisted phone numbers were included in the sample, the last two digits of the phone numbers selected in the first step were replaced by numbers generated randomly by a computer.

In the public opinion survey, interviewers used the approach developed by Hagen and Collier (1982) and selected a respondent at random once telephone contact was made. Respondents had to be eighteen years old or older and had to live in the Keys at least nine months out of the year. In the lot owner survey, the interviewers asked if anyone in the household owned an undeveloped lot in the Keys, and if the response was affirmative, the interviewer simply asked to speak with someone in the household who was knowledgeable about the lot(s). The samples of telephone numbers were purchased from Survey Sampling, Inc. The response rates were calculated by dividing the number of completed interviews by the number of working telephone numbers in the sample. The response rates for the 1984, 1985, and 1986 public opinion surveys were, respectively, 72.5 percent, 66.3 percent, and 69.1 percent. The response rate for the lot owner survey was 12 percent. The response rate was low in the lot owner survey because, as discussed later, only about 15 percent of the households owned undeveloped lots.

2. The exact wording was, "In your view, is the quality of the natural environment in the Keys getting better, getting worse, or not changing?"

3. The exact wording was, "Generally, would you favor relaxing land use regulations to permit more development, strengthening land use regulations to reduce development or improve its quality, or leaving land use regulations pretty much as they are now?"

4. The questions were: "Have you heard about the new land use Plan for Monroe County that was adopted last spring by the county commission? (IF YES:) Do you personally favor the new plan, do you oppose it, are you not sure, or do you not really care about it one way or the other?"

5. The exact wording was: "All right, what about the proposed tourist impact tax that was also on the ballot? Did you vote for or against the tourist impact tax?"

6. Questions on the commision races were: "In the race between Mike Puto and Allison Fahrer, did you vote for Puto or for Fahrer? In the race between Jerry Hernandez and Coakley Allen, did you vote for Hernandez or for Allen? In the race between Gene Lytton and Vern Pokorski, did you vote for Lytton or for Pokorski?"

7. The questions were: "All right, let me ask you a few questions about the Plan. There are a number of things about the Plan that some people have told us are big problems and others have said we should not worry about. We would like to start with the possibility that the Plan might hurt the local economy. Do you personally think that the Plan's effect on the local economy is a big problem, or that it's not a big problem? All right, what about how the Plan affects the property rights of people who own undeveloped lots in the Keys? In your view, is the Plan's effect on property rights a big problem, or is it not a big problem? OK, what about the possibility that the Plan might cause the cost of housing to go way up? Do you personally think that the Plan's effect on the cost of housing in the Keys is a big problem, or is it not a big problem? All right, what about the possibility that the Plan may not provide enough protection of the natural environment? In your view, is the possibility that the Plan

may not provide enough protection of the natural environment a big problem, or is it not a big problem? OK, what about the possibility that the Plan will allow too much development and construction in the Keys? Do you personally think that the amount of development allowed by the Plan is a big problem, or is it not a big problem? All right. Thinking now about how the Plan affects different groups in the Keys—how it affects residents, land owners, taxpayers, different businesses, and so on—overall, would you say that the Plan is fair in how it affects different groups, or that it's not fair, or are you uncertain about this? All right, one more question about the Plan. Thinking about your job or career, the value of any land or housing you might own, and other things of concern to you that the Plan might affect, overall, would you say that the Plan will probably hurt you, that it will help you, or that its pluses and minuses for you personally pretty much balance out?"

References

Albrecht, D. E., G. Bultena, and E. Hoiberg (1986). "Constituency of the Antigrowth Movement: A Comparison of the Growth Orientations of Urban Status Groups." *Urban Affairs Quarterly* 21: 607–16.

Althoff, P., and W. H. Creig (1977). "Environmental Pollution Control: Two Views from the General Population." *Environment and Behavior* 9:441–56.

Anthony, R. (1982). "Polls, Pollution and Politics: Trends in Public Opinion on the Environment." *Environment,* pp. 4–20.

Arbuthnot, J., and S. Lingg (1975). "A Comparison of French and American Environmental Behaviors, Knowledge and Attitudes." *International Journal of Psychology* 10:275–81.

Ash, R. (1972). *Social Movements in America*. Chicago: Markham Publishing Co.

Babcock, R. F. (1966). *The Zoning Game*. Madison: University of Wisconsin Press.

Babcock, R. F., and C. L. Siemon (1985). *The Zoning Game Revisited*. Boston: Lincoln Institute of Land Policy.

Baldassare, M. (1984). "Predicting Local Concern About Growth: The Roots of Citizen Discontent." *Journal of Urban Affairs,* pp. 39–49.

Bennett, S. E. (1973). "Consistency Among the Public's Social Welfare Policy Attitudes in the 1960s." *American Journal of Political Science* 17:544–70.

Blalock, H. M., Jr. (1979). *Social Statistics*. New York: McGraw-Hill.

Block, M. (1983). "Florida's Amendment 1 Citizens' Choice on Government Revenue: Facts, Fallacies and Philosophies." Mimeo.

Borden, R. J., and J. L. Francis (1978). "Who Cares About Ecology? Personality and Sex Differences in Environmental Concern." *Journal of Personality* 46:190–203.

Boskin, M. J. (1979). "Some Neglected Economic Factors Behind Recent Tax and Spending Limitation Movements." *National Tax Journal* 32:37–42.

Bosselman, F., and D. Callies (1972). *The Quiet Revolution in Land Use Control.* Washington, D.C.: U.S. Government Printing Office.

Bowman, F. H. (1977). "Public Opinion and the Environment: Post-Earth Day Attitudes Among College Students." *Environment and Behavior* 9:385–416.

Buttel, F. H., and D. E. Johnson (1977). "Dimensions of Environmental Concern: Factor Structure, Correlates, and Implications for Research." *Journal of Environmental Education* 9:49–64.

Buttel, F. H., and W. L. Flinn (1974). "The Structure of Support for the Environmental Movement, 1968–1970." *Rural Sociology* 39:56–69.

———. (1976a). "Economic Growth Versus the Environment: Survey Evidence." *Social Science Quarterly* 57:410–20.

———. (1976b). "Environmental Politics: The Structuring of Partisan and Ideological Cleavages in Mass Environmental Attitudes." *Sociology Quarterly* 17:477–90.

———. (1978a). "The Politics of Environmental Concern: The Impacts of Party Identification and Political Ideology on Environmental Attitudes." *Environment and Behavior* 10:433–50.

———. (1978b). "Social Class and Mass Environmental Beliefs: A Reconsideration." *Environment and Behavior* 10:433–50.

Campbell, A., P. E. Converse, W. E. Miller, and D. E. Stokes (1960). *The American Voter.* Chicago: Rand-McNally.

Campbell, D. T., and D. W. Fiske (1959). "Convergent and Discriminant Validation by the Multi-trait, Multi-method Matrix." *Psychology Bulletin* 56:81–105.

Carter, L. J. (1979). "Public Support for Environmental Protection Remains Strong." *Science* 203:154.

Citrin, J. (1979). "Do People Want Something for Nothing?: Public Opinion on Taxes and Government Spending." *National Tax Journal* 32 (Supplement): 113–30.

Cline, R. J., and J. Shannon (1982). "Municipal Revenue Behavior After Proposition 13." *Intergovernmental Perspective* 8: n.p.

Coleman, R. P. (1959). "Social Class in Kansas City." Ph.D. diss., University of Chicago.

Colman, W. G. (1983). "A Quiet Revolution in Local Government Finance: Policy and Administrative Challenges in Expanding the Role of User Charges in Financing State and Local Government." Washington, D.C.: National Academy of Public Administration.

Connerly, C. E. (1986). "Growth Management Concern: The Impact of Its Definition on Support for Local Growth Controls." *Environment and Behavior* 18:707–32.

Consensus Estimating Conference (1983). *Citizens' Choice Amendment 1: Impact on Florida State Revenues.* Tallahassee, Fla.: Office of the Secretary of the Senate.

Converse, P. E. (1964). "The Nature of Belief Systems in Mass Publics." In *Ideology and Discontent,* edited by D. E. Apter. New York: The Free Press.

References

———. (1973). "Public Opinion and Voting Behavior." *Nongovernmental Politics* 4:124–25.

Council on Environmental Quality (1981). *Environmental Quality 1981*. Washington, D.C.: U.S. Government Printing Office.

Craik, K. H., and G. E. McKechinie (1977). "Personality and Environment." *Environment and Behavior* 9:155–68.

Cronbach, L. J. (1960). *Essentials of Psychological Testing*. New York: Harper.

Cutter, S. C. (1981). "Community Concern for Pollution: Social and Environmental Influences." *Environment and Behavior* 13:105–24.

DeGroot, I. (1967). "Trends in Public Attitudes Toward Air Pollution." *Journal of Air Pollution Control Association*. 17:679–81.

DeGrove, J. M. (1984). *Land, Growth & Politics*. Chicago: American Planning Association.

deHaven-Smith, L. (1984a). "Concern Over Waste in Government: The Attitudes of Palm Beach County Residents on Florida's Taxes and Services." *Florida Environmental and Urban Issues* 11 (April): 6–13.

———. (1984b). "How to Calculate the Revenue Limit from Amendment 1." *Florida Environmental and Urban Issues* 11 (January): 26–30.

———. (1984c). "Overwhelming Support for Land-Use Controls: The Attitudes of Monroe County Residents on Growth Management Issues." *Florida Environmental and Urban Issues* 12 (October): 4–11.

———. (1984d). "Regulatory Theory and State Land-Use Regulation: Implications from Florida's Experience with Growth Management." *Public Administration Review* 5 (September/October): 413–20.

———. (1985a). "The Attitudes of Lee County Voters on Growth Management Issues." *Florida Environmental and Urban Issues* 11 (January).

———. (1985b). "Ideology and the Tax Revolt: Florida's Amendment 1." *Public Opinion Quarterly* 49:300–309.

———. (1985c) "Special Districts: A Structural Approach to Infrastructure Finance and Management." In *The Changing Structure of Infrastructure Finance*, Monograph 85-5, edited by James C. Nicholas. Cambridge, Mass.: Lincoln Institute of Land Policy.

———. (1987). *Environmental Publics: Public Opinion on Environmental Protection and Growth Management*. Boston: Lincoln Institute of Land Policy.

———. (1988a). "Environmental Belief Systems: Public Opinion toward Land Use Regulation in Florida." *Environment and Behavior* 20:176–99.

———. (1988b). *Philosophical Critiques of Policy Analysis: Lindblom, Habermas, and the Great Society*. Gainesville: University of Florida Press.

———. (1989). "Toward a Communicative Theory of Environmental Opinion: A Rejoinder to Audirac and Shoemyen." *Environment and Behavior* 21 (September): 630–35.

deHaven-Smith, L., and D. S. Gatlin (1985). "The Florida Voter: A Regional Analysis." *Florida Geographer* 19 (September).

Dillman, D. A. (1978). *Mail and Telephone Surveys, The Total Design Method.* New York: John Wiley.

Dillman, D. A., and J. A. Christenson (1972). "The Public Value for Pollution Control." In *Social Behavior, Natural Resources and the Environment,* edited by W. R. Burch, Jr., N. H. Cheek, Jr., and L. Taylor. New York: Harper and Row.

Dispoto, R. G. (1977). "Interrelationships Among Measures of Environmental Activity, Emotionality, and Knowledge." *Education and Psychology Measurement* 37:451–59.

Downs, A. (1972). "Up and Down with Ecology." *The Public Interest* 28 (Summer):38–50.

Dunlap, R. E. (1975). "The Impact of Political Orientation on Environmental Attitudes and Actions." *Environment and Behavior.* 7:428–54.

Dunlap, R. E., and M. P. Allen (1976). "Partisan Differences on Environmental Issues: A Congressional Roll-call Analysis." *Western Political Quarterly* 29:384–97.

Dunlap, R. E., R. P. Gale, and B. M. Rutherford (1973). "Concern for Environmental Rights Among College Students." *American Journal of Economics and Sociology* 32:45–60.

Dunlap, R. E., J. K. Grineeks, and M. Rokeach (1975). "Human Values and Pro-Environmental Values." Paper presented at the annual meeting of the Pacific Sociological Association, Victoria, B.C.

Dunlap, R. E., and K. D. Van Liere (1978). *Environmental Concern: A Bibliography of Empirical Studies and Brief Appraisal of the Literature.* Public Administration Series Bibliography No. 44. Monticello, Ill.: Vance Bibliographies.

―――. (1980). "Commitment to the Dominant Social Paradigm and Support for Ecological Policies: An Empirical Analysis." Revision of a paper presented at the meeting of the Society for the Study of Social Problems, San Francisco, 1978.

Dunlap, R. E., K. D. Van Liere, and D. A. Dillman (1979). "Evidence of Decline in Public Concern with Environmental Quality." *Rural Sociology.* 44:204–12.

Erskine, H. (1972a). "The Polls: Pollution and its Costs." *Public Opinion Quarterly* (Spring): 120–35.

―――. (1972b). The Polls: Pollution and Industry." *Public Opinion Quarterly* (Summer): 263–80.

Field, J. O., and R. E. Anderson (1969). "Ideology in the Public's Conceptualization of the 1964 Election." *Public Opinion Quarterly* 33:380–98.

Florida Advisory Council on Intergovernmental Relations (1984). *Citizens Choice Amendment 1: Impact on Counties, Municipalities and Independent Special Districts.* Tallahassee, Fla.

Florida Statistical Abstract (1985). Gainesville: University of Florida Press.

Gallup Report (1982). *Political, Social and Economic Trends.* Report No. 206. November.

Grossman, G. M. and H. R. Potter (1977a). "A Longitudinal Analysis of Environmental Concern: Evidence from National Surveys." Paper presented at the annual meeting of the American Sociological Association, Chicago.

———. (1977b). "A Trend Analysis of Competing Models of Environmental Attitudes." Working paper no. 127, Institute for the Study of Social Change, Department of Sociology and Anthropology, Purdue University.

Hagen, D. E., and C. M. Collier (1982). "Respondent Selection Procedures for Telephone Surveys: Must They Be Intrusive?" Paper presented at the annual conference of the American Association for Public Opinion Research, Baltimore.

Harris, Louis and Associates, Inc. (1970a). *The Public's View of Environmental Problems in the State of Oregon*. New York: Louis Harris and Associates.

———. (1970b). *The Public's View of Environmental Problems in the State of Washington*. New York: Louis Harris and Associates.

Harry, J. (1971). "Work and Leisure: Situational Attitudes." *Pacific Sociological Review* 14:302–9.

Hausknecht, M. (1962). *The Joiners: A Sociological Description of Voluntary Association Membership in the United States*. New York: Bedminster.

Healy, R. G. (1976). *Land Use and the States*. Washington, D.C.: Resources for the Future, Inc.

Heberlein, T. A. (1977). "Norm Activation and Environmental Action." *Journal of Social Issues* 3:207–11.

Hornback, K. E. (1974). "Orbits of Opinion: The Role of Age in the Environmental Movement's Attentive Public." Ph.D. diss., Michigan State University.

Horvat, R. E., and A. M. Voelker (1976). "Using Likert Scale to Measure Environmental Responsibility." *Journal of Environmental Education* 8:36–47.

Kay, David A., and Harold K. Jacobson (1983). *Environmental Protection*. Totoa, N.J.: Allanheld, Osmun & Co.

Kelling, G. W. (1970). "Problems of Sampling for Non-Demographic and Composition Variables in a Moderate-Sized City." Paper presented at a meeting of the Rocky Mountain Psychological Association, Salt Lake City.

Key, V. O. (1966). *The Responsible Electorate*. Cambridge: Harvard University Press.

Kirlin, J. J. (1982). *The Political Economy of Fiscal Limits*. Lexington, Mass.: Lexington Books.

Koenig. D. J. (1975). "Additional Research on Environmental Activism." *Environment and Behavior* 7:472–85.

Kronus, C. L., and J. C. Van Es (1976). "The Practice of Environmental Quality Behavior." *Journal of Environmental Education* 8:19–25.

Labovitz, S., and R. Hagedorn (1976). *Introduction to Social Research*. 2d ed. New York: McGraw-Hill.

Ladd, E. C., Jr., with Marilyn Potter, Linda Basilick, Sally Daniels, and Dana Suszkiw (1979). "The Polls: Taxing and Spending." *Public Opinion Quarterly* 43:126–35.

Lane, R. E. (1962). *Political Ideology*. New York: The Free Press.

Levy, F. (1979). "On Understanding Proposition 13." *The Public Interest* 56:66–89.

Lipset, S. M., and W. Schneider (1980). "Is the Tax Revolt Over?" *Taxing and Spending* 3(Summer): 73–78.

Lounsbury, J. W., and L. G. Tornatzky (1977). "A Scale for Assessing Attitudes Toward Environmental Quality." *Journal of Social Psychology* 101:299–305.

Lowenthal, D. (1972). "Research in Environmental Perceptions and Behavior: Perspectives on Current Problems." *Environment and Behavior* 4:333–42.

Luttbeg, N. (1968). "The Structure of Beliefs Among Leaders and the Public." *Public Opinion Quarterly* 32:398–409.

McCarney, P. L. (1983). "Increasing Reliance on User Fees and Charges." In *Proposition 2½: Its Impacts on Massachusetts*, edited by Lawrence E. Susskind and Jane Fountain Serio. Cambridge, Mass.: Oelgeschlager, Gunn, and Hain.

McClosky, H. (1964). "Consensus and Ideology in American Politics." *American Political Science Review* 58:361–82.

McEvoy, J., III (1972). "The American Concern with the Environment." In *Social Behavior, Natural Resources and the Environment*, edited by W. R. Burch, Jr., N. H. Cheek, Jr., and L. Taylor. New York: Harper and Row.

McKechnie, G. E. (1977). "The Environmental Response Inventory in Application." *Environment and Behavior* 9:255–76.

Malkis, A., and H. G. Grasmick (1977). "Support for the Ideology of the Environmental Movement: Tests of Alternative Hypothesis." *Western Sociological Review* 8:25–47.

Maloney, M. P., and M. P. Ward (1973). "Ecology: Let's Hear from the People." *American Psychologist* 28:583–86.

Mannheim, K. (1952). "The Problem of Generations." In *Essays on the Sociology of Knowledge*. New York: Oxford University Press.

Marsh, C. P., and J. A. Christenson (1977). "Support for Economic Growth and Environmental Protection, 1973–1975." *Rural Sociology* 42:101–7.

Martison, O. B., and E. A. Wilkening (1975). "A Scale to Measure Awareness of Environmental Problems: Structure and Correlates." Paper presented at the annual meeting of the Midwest Sociological Society, Chicago.

Maslow, A. H. (1970). *Motivation and Personality.* 2d ed. New York: Viking Press.

Medler, J., and A. Mushkatel (1979). "Urban-Rural Class Conflict in Oregon Land-Use Planning." *Western Political Quarterly* 32:338–49.

Milbrath, L. W. (1965). *Political Participation*. Chicago: Rand McNally.

Mitchell, R. C. (1979). "Silent Spring/Solid Majorities." *Public Opinion* 2:16–20, 55.

Morrison, D. E., K. E. Hornback, and W. K. Warner (1973). "The Environmental Movement: Some Preliminary Observations and Predictions." In *Social Behavior, Natural Resources and the Environment*, edited by W. R. Burch, Jr., N. H. Cheek, Jr., and L. Taylor. New York: Harper and Row.

Murch, A. W. (1974). "Who Cares About the Environment?: The Nature and

Origins of Environmental Concern." In *Environmental Concern,* edited by A. W. Murch. New York: MSS Information Corporation.

———. (1971). "Public Concern for Environmental Pollution." *Public Opinion Quarterly* (Spring):100–106.

Murdock, S. H., and E. C. Schriner (1977). "Social and Economic Determinants of the Level of Support for Environmental Protection and Economic Growth in a Rural Population." Paper presented at the annual meeting of the Rural Sociological Society, Madison, Wisconsin.

Natchez, P. B. (1985). *Images of Voting/Visions of Democracy.* New York: Basic Books.

National Wildlife Federation (1969). "The U.S. Public Considers Its Environment," Report of the national survey conducted by Gallup International, Inc., Washington, D.C.

———. (1970). "A Study of the Attitudes of the American Public Toward Improvement of the Natural Environment." Report of the national survey conducted by L. Harris and Associates, Washington, D.C.

———. (1981). "Environment Is Still Important to Most Americans." January.

New York Times (1981). "Poll Finds Strong Support for Environmental Code." 4 October.

New York Times (1981). "Public Prefers a Balanced Budget to Large Cut in Taxes." 3 February.

Nie, N., with C. Andersen (1974). "Mass Belief Systems Revisited: Political Change and Attitude Structure." *Journal of Politics.* 36:540–91.

Niemi, R. G., R. D. Ross, and J. Alexander (1978). "The Similarity of Political Values of Parents and College-age Youths." *Public Opinion Quarterly* 43:503–20.

Nunnaly, J. C. (1967) *Psychometric Theory.* New York: McGraw-Hill.

Ogden, D. M., Jr. (1971). "The Future of the Environmental Struggle." In *The Politics of Neglect,* edited by R. L. Meek and J. A. Straayer. Boston: Houghton Mifflin.

O'Hare, M., L. Bacow, and D. Sanderson, (1983). *Facility Siting and Public Opposition.* New York: Van Nostrand Reinhold.

Parker, S. L., and A. Oppenheim (1986). *The 1986 Florida Annual Policy Survey: Policy Preferences and Priorities of the Florida Public.* Florida State University, Policy Sciences Program.

Passino, E. M., and J. W. Lounsbury (1976). "Sex Differences in Opposition to and Support for Construction of a Proposed Nuclear Power Plant." In *The Behavioral Basis of Design,* Book 1, edited by M. Ward, S. Coren, A. Gruft, and J. B. Collins. Stroudsburg, Penn.: Dowden, Hutchinson and Ross.

Pelham, T. G. (1979). *State Land-Use Planning and Regulation.* Lexington, Mass.: D.C. Heath and Company.

Peretz, P. (1982). "There Was No Tax Revolt!" *Politics and Society* 11:231–49.

Pfiffner, J. P. (1983). "Inflexible Budgets, Fiscal Stress, and the Tax Revolt." In *The*

Municipal Money Chase, edited by A. M. Sbragia, 37–66. Boulder, Colo.: Westview Press.

Pierce, J. C. (1970). "Party Identification and the Changing Role of Ideology in American Politics." *Midwest Journal of Political Science* 16:25–42.

―――. (1979). "Water Resource Preservation: Personal Values and Public Support." *Environment and Behavior* 11:147–61.

Pierce. J. C., and N. P. Lorvrich, Jr. (1980). "Belief Systems Concerning the Environment: The General Public, Attentive Publics, and State Legislators." *Political Behavior* 2:259–86.

Pomper, G. M. (1972). "From Confusion to Clarity: Issues and American Voters, 1956–1968." *American Political Science Review* 66:415–28.

Popper, F. J. (1987). "The Environmentalists and the LULU." In *Resolving Locational Conflict*, edited by R. W. Lake. New Brunswick, N.J.: Center for Urban Policy Research, Rutgers University.

Prothro, J. W., and C. M. Grigg (1960). "Fundamental Principles of Democracy: Bases of Agreement and Disagreement." *Journal of Politics* 22:276–94.

RePass, D. E. (1971) "Issues Salience and Party Choice." *American Political Science Review* 65:389–400.

Sabatier, P. A. (1974). "State and Local Policy: A Modest Review of Past Efforts and Future Topics." In *Environmental Politics*, edited by S. S. Nagel. New York: Praeger.

Schuman, H., and M. D. Johnson (1976). "Attitudes and Behavior." *Annual Review of Sociology* 2:161–207.

Seley, J. E. (1983). *The Politics of Public-Facility Planning*. Lexington, Mass.: D. C. Heath.

Sharma, N. C., J. E. Kivlin, and F. C. Fliegel (1975). "Environmental Pollution: Is There Enough Public Concern to Lead to Action?" *Environment and Behavior* 7:455–71.

Sigo, S. (1986). "Commissioners See New Direction." *The Keynoter* (9 November): 4, 6.

Simon, R. J. (1972). "Public Attitudes Toward Population and Pollution." *Public Opinion Quarterly* (Summer): 93–99.

Smith, Jim (1983). "Attorney General Opinion Number 83–64." Tallahassee, Fla.: Department of Legal Affairs.

Springer, J. F., and E. Constantini (1974). "Public Opinion and the Environment: An Issue in Search of a Home." In *Environmental Politics*, edited by S. S. Nagel. New York: Praeger.

Stallings, R. A. (1973). "Patterns of Belief in Social Movements: Clarifications from an Analysis of Environmental Groups." *The Sociological Quarterly* 14:465–80.

Susskind, L., and C. Horan (1983). "Understanding How and Why the Most Drastic Cuts Were Avoided." In *Proposition 2½: Its Impact on Massachusetts*, edited by Lawrence E. Susskind and Jane Fountain Serio, 263–91.

Swan, J. A. (1971). "Environmental Education: One Approach to Resolving the Environmental Crisis." *Environment and Behavior* 3:223–29.

Tittle, C. R., and R. J. Hill (1967). "The Accuracy of Self-Reported Data and Prediction of Political Activity." *Public Opinion Quarterly* 31:103–6.

Toch, H. (1965). *The Social Psychology of Social Movements*. New York: Bobbs-Merrill.

Tognacci, L. N., R. H. Weigel, M. F. Wideen, and D. T. A. Vernon (1972). "Environmental Quality: How Universal is Public Concern?" *Environment and Behavior* 4:73–86.

Trembley, K. R., Jr., and R. E. Dunlap (1978). "Rural Residence and Concern with Environmental Quality: A Replication and Extension." *Rural Sociology* 43: 474–91.

Udall, S., and J. Stansbury (1971). "The SST Issue—Davis vs Goliath." *Denver Post* (15 March): 22.

U. S. News and World Report (1978). "When People Speak Out on Today's Issues." 13 February, pp. 37–40.

Utrup, K. (1981) "Public Opinion and Environmental Protection." *Sierra*, p. 13.

Van Liere, K. D., and R. E. Dunlap (1978). "Environmental Concern: Consistency Among Its Dimensions, Conceptualizations and Empirical Correlates." Paper presented at the annual meeting of the Pacific Sociological Association, Spokane, Washington.

———. (1980). "The Social Bases of Environmental Concern: A Review of Hypotheses, Explanations and Empirical Evidence." *Public Opinion Quarterly* (Summer): 181–97.

———. (1981). "Environmental Concern: Does It Make A Difference How It Is Measured." *Environment and Behavior* 13(6): 651–76.

Wall, G. (1973). "Public Response to Air Pollution in South Yorkshire, England." *Environment and Behavior* 5:219–48.

Webber, D. J. (1982). "Is Nuclear Power Just Another Environmental Issue? An Analysis of California Voters." *Environment and Behavior* 14:72–83.

Weigel, R. H. (1977). "Ideological and Demographic Correlates of Proecology Behavior." *Journal of Social Psychology* 103:39–47.

Weigel, R. H., and L. S. Newman (1976) "Increasing Attitude-Behavior Correspondence by Broadening the Scope of the Behavior Measure." *Journal of Personality and Social Psychology* 33:793–802.

Weigel, R. H., and J. Weigel (1978). "Environmental Concern: The Development of a Measure." *Environment and Behavior* 10:3–15.

Wilson, J. (1973). *Introduction to Social Movements*. New York: Basic Books.

Wolfinger, R. E., Barbara Kay Wolfinger, Kenneth Prewitt, and Sheilah Rosenhack (1964). "America's Radical Right: Politics and Ideology." In *Ideology and Discontent*, edited by D. E. Apter, 262–93. New York: The Free Press.

Zingale, J. (1984). "Fiscal Analysis of the Immediate Impact of Amendment 1 on State Revenues." *Florida Environmental and Urban Issues* 11(January): 23–26.

Index

Agriculture: attitudes toward, 42–44, 95; questions for measuring attitudes toward, 119n.4
Aid to the poor, attitudes toward, 71–73
Airports, attitudes toward, 73–76, 78–79
Alachua County, 28
Area of Critical State Concern (ACSC): designation of Florida Keys as, 82–84; legislative changes in, 83–84; program described, 27
Army Corps of Engineers, 59
Ash, Roberta, 4
Attenuation theory: alternatives to, 79–81; conceptual inadequacies of, 67; described, 66–67; evidential inadequacies of, 67; policy implications of, 66; and tax revolt, 66–67
Audubon Society, 34

Billboards, attitudes toward, 39–41, 95
Blalock, H. M., Jr., 123n.7
Broward County, 28
Buffet, Jimmy, 25
Buildings: attitudes toward, 95; attitudes toward height of, 62; attitudes toward location of, 62–63; questions for measuring attitudes toward, 121n.12, 122n.15
Built environment, 39–41, 47; and quality of life, 26

California, 21
Citrus County, 28
Coalitions: effects of policies on, 95–96; and issue publics, 80–81, 88–90; and policy concepts, 98; splintering of, 92
Conceptualization: and attitudes toward Proposition 1, 69–70; in mass belief systems, 6; and service preferences, 70–73
Concern for pollution, viii; trends of, 1
Conflict theory, 4
Consistency: and elite discourse, 8; and mass belief systems, 6
Constraint: and conceptualization of environmental problems, 42–44; and environmental belief systems, 41–45; and mass belief systems, 6–8

Index

Converse, Philip E., 23, 31, 39, 97; criticisms of, 7–8; and the locus of environmental concern, 15; theory of public opinion, 5–8
Crime: attitudes toward, 50–53, 62, 78–79; demographic correlates of attitudes toward, 51; questions for measuring attitudes toward, 119n.2, 121n.12
Crocodiles, 25

Dade County, 28
Daytona Beach, 28
Delray Beach, 49; attitudes toward building heights in, 62; attitudes toward land use regulation in, 60–61; development patterns in, 63; elite discourse in, 60, 63; fear of overdevelopment in, 62–63; perceptions of public problems in, 60–62; perceptions of quality of life in, 61; population growth in, 59
Demographic factors: and attitudes toward land use regulation, 55, 61; and attitudes toward planning, 87; and attitudes toward Proposition 1, 69, 72–73; and attitudes toward public problems, 51; and perceptions of environmental problems, 57
Density, questions for measuring attitudes toward, 118n.4
Development, attitudes toward, 39–41
Development of Regional Impact, defined, 27, 116n.5
Development patterns: in Delray Beach, 63; and environmental concern, 64–65; in Lee County, 63; response of elites to, 64; in Sunrise, 63
Douglas, Marjory Stoneman, 116n.3
Downs, Anthony, 2
Downzoning, of Florida Keys, 85

Eagles, 25
Economic development: attitudes toward, 30–34, 58; in Lee County, 58; questions for measuring attitudes toward, 117n.8
Economic growth, attitudes toward, 30–34, 42–44
Economic issues, attitudes toward, 16
Elite discourse: contrasted with mass opinion, 7; in Delray Beach, 60, 63; effects on environmental concern, 19–21, 35, 48, 93–94; effects on opinion, 97; effects on perceptions of problems, 95–96; and environmental concern, 9–12; and environmental opinion in Florida, 33–35; in Indian River County, 39; and issue publics, 7–8; in Lee County, 55–56, 63; in St. Lucie County, 39; in Sunrise, Florida, 63; in the Treasure Coast region, 37–39
Endangered species, in Florida, 25–26
Environmental belief systems: and conceptualization of environmental problems, 36, 39–41, 47; and constraint, 41–45; and elite discourse, 36; and environmental problems, 32–35; foundations of, 46–47; organization of attitudes in, 33–35; range of, 23, 33–35, 47
Environmental concern: and attenuation theory, 66–67; and attitudes toward land use regulation, 57–58; compared to other concerns, 2, 16–17; conceptions of, vii, 1–3, 27–28; demographic correlates of, 9, 57–58, 97; effects of development patterns on, 64–65; and elite discourse, 9–12, 19–21, 48, 93–94; and environmental policy, 80–81; and environmental problems, 8–9, 33–35, 47; fragmented nature of, 9,

33, 35–36, 80–81, 97; intrastate variation of, 27–29; and issue attention cycle, 2; as measured by Gallup, 1; as measured by Roper, 2–3; measures of, viii, 16, 21–22, 31; narrowness of, 95; and policy positions, 13; as a policy process, 93–94; and population growth, 64–65; and public opinion theory, 33–34; questions about, 12; referent of, 12, 16–17, 36, 47; in select states, 18–19; stability of, 2–3; strategies for mobilizing, 9; strength of, 2–3; trends of, 1–3; and uglification, 39–41; and visibility principle, 64–65, 95
Environmental groups, conflict between, in Florida, 34
Environmental movement: approaches to analysis of, 21–22; and attitude scaling, viii; and conceptions of environmental concern, 1–3; and conflict theory, 4; and environmental concern, 93–94; future of, 98–99; nature of, 98; as a new social movement, 4–5; and structural functionalism, 3–4
Environmental opinion: conditions causing polarization of, 64–65; volatility of, 80–81
Environmental policy: directed toward local problems, 16–21; effects on coalitions, 95–96; and environmental concern, 93–94; in Florida, 26–27; possible criteria for evaluating, 67
Environmental problems: and attitudes toward land use regulation, 57–58; and attitudes in Lee County, 57–58; conceptualization of, 36, 47; effects on environmental belief systems, 32–35; effects on environmental concern, 47; in Florida, 25–26; perceptions of, 49, 87–88, 95–96; questions for measuring perceptions of, 120n.7
Environmental risk, questions for measuring attitudes toward, 118n.4
Everglades, deer hunting in, 34
Expressways: attitudes toward, 73–76; questions for measuring attitudes toward, 124n.10

Florida: attitudes toward crime in, 51; environmental problems in, 25–26, 33; growth management policies of, 13, 21, 26–27; growth management problems of, 13; panhandle of, 28; population growth in, 23–25
Florida Conservation Association, 34
Florida Department of Community Affairs, 27, 59
Florida Keys, 54; ACSC designation of, 82–84; adoption of plan for, 84–86; downzoning of, 84–85; geography of, 82–83; land authority in, 86; lot ownership in, 85; perceptions of environmental problems in, 87; platted subdivisions in, 84–85; population growth in, 83
Florida panther, 25–26
Florida Wildlife Federation, 34
Focus groups, 97
Foreign policy, attitudes toward, 16–17
Fort Lauderdale, 49
Fort Myers, 55
Friends of the Everglades, 34

Gallup surveys: inaccuracy of, 21; measures of environmental concern in, 1–2
Gamma, characteristics of, 31
Goss, Porter, 56
Government, attitudes toward, 16, 53–54, 78–79

Index

Growth management: attitudes toward, 9, 30–34, 98; as a coalition concept, 96; in Florida, 26–27; policies in the Treasure Coast Region, 37–39; states with policies for, 21
Growth management concern, viii

Hawaii, 21
Health care, attitudes toward, 70–73
Housing costs: perceptions of, in Delray Beach, 62; questions for measuring attitudes toward, 121n.12

Idea-elements, in mass belief systems, 7
Ideologues: and attitudes toward Proposition 1, 69–70; defined, 6; percentage of mass public, 6
Impact fees, 37
Income, in Lee County, 58
Indian River County, 37, 46; elite discourse in, 39
Issue publics: defined, 7; and elite discourse, 8, 34–35; environmental, 13, 17, 30–35, 47, 95–96; and environmental problems, 91–92; in Florida, 33–35, 47; in Florida Keys, 88–90; and growth management, 88; in Lee County, 58–59; measures of, 17; and opinion toward LULUs, 77–80; in Palm Beach County, 77–79; and planning, 91–92; response of, to policy changes, 91–92; shifting coalitions of, 88–90; volatility of, 33–35, 80–81, 91–92, 95–96

Land authority, in Florida Keys, 86
Landfills: attitudes toward, 78–79; questions for measuring attitudes toward, 124n.10
Landscaping, attitudes toward, 39–41

Land use regulation: attitudes toward, 30–34, 39–41, 47, 54–56, 60–61; and attitudes toward economic development, 58; attitudes toward and perceptions of environmental problems, 57–58; demographic correlates of attitudes toward, 55, 61; and perceptions of different levels of government, 59, 121n.9; and perceptions of environmental problems, 57–58; questions for measuring attitudes toward, 36–37, 117n.8, 118n.2, 121n.9, 126n.3
Lee County, 49, 55–60; attitudes toward land use regulation in, 56; average income in, 58; development patterns in, 63; and economic development, 58; elite discourse in, 55–56, 63; natural beauty of, 57; perceptions of environmental problems in, 57–58, population growth in, 55
Locally unwanted land uses (LULUs): attitudes toward, 73–76; defined, 67; and issue publics, 78–80; in Palm Beach County, 73–74; prevailing theory of, 122n.1
Lot ownership: effect on attitudes, 87; in Florida Keys, 85

Manatees, 25
Marion County, 28
Martin County, 37, 47
Mass belief systems: communication and, 10–12, 97; characteristics of, 6–8; and elite discourse, 8; globularity of, 11; and issue publics, 7; and mass opinion, 11; and voting, 7
Mass communication, and environmental concern, 97
Monroe County, 28

New Jersey, 21
New social movements theory, 4–5; and locus of environmental concern, 15
Not-in-my-back-yard (NIMBY) theory, 14, 122n.1; alternatives to, 79–80; critique of, 79–80; defined, 67; test of, 76–79
Nuclear power, attitudes toward, 9
Nuclear power concern, viii

O'Hare, M., 122n.1
1,000 Friends of Florida, 38
Open-ended questions, criticisms of, 41–42
Open space: perceptions of, in Delray Beach, 62; questions for measuring attitudes toward, 121n.12
Oregon, 21
Orlando, 28
Overpopulation, attitudes toward, 9

Palm Beach County, 28, 37, 46; attitudes toward Proposition 1 in, 69; issue publics in, 77–79; test of NIMBY theory in, 76–79
Panthers, 34
Planning: attitudes toward, 39–44, 46, 87–88; in Delray Beach, 60; in Florida, 26–27; in Florida Keys, 84–86; and issue publics, 91–92; in Lee County, 55–56; questions for measuring attitudes toward, 126n.4, 126n.7
Pollution: attitudes toward, 9, 30–33, 39–41, 95, 97; in Florida, 25; questions for measuring attitudes toward, 117n.8
Popper, F. J., 122n.1
Population growth: attitudes toward, 77–78; and attitudes toward LULUs, 77–80; in Delray Beach, 59; effects of, on environmental concern, 64–65; in Florida, 23–24, 116n.2; in Florida Keys, 83; in Lee County, 55; in Sunrise, Florida, 50; and tax revolt, 66–67; in Treasure Coast Region, 37
Principle of overriding interests: defined, 80; implications of, 80–81, 94–95
Proposition 1: conceptualization of, 70; and demographic factors, 69, 72–73; described, 68; expected impacts from, 68–69; opinion toward, 69; and preferences for public services, 70–73; question for measuring attitudes toward, 123n.3
Public opinion theory: and environmental concern, 33–34; challenges of, to sociology, 5
Public problems: attitudes toward, 50–53; perceptions of, in Delray Beach, 61–62; questions for measuring attitudes toward, 119n.3
Public safety, attitudes toward, 71–73
Public services: attitudes toward, 53; and attitudes toward Proposition 1, 70–73; questions for measuring attitudes toward, 119n.5
Putnam County, 28

Quality of life: deterioration of, in Florida, 26; perceptions of, in Delray Beach, 61
Questions for measuring attitudes toward: agriculture, 118n.4; buildings, 121n.12, 122n.15; crime, 119n.2, 121n.12; density, 118n.4; economic development, 117n.8; environmental problems, 120n.7; environmental risk, 118n.4; expressways, 124n.10; housing costs, 121n.12; landfills, 124n.10; land use regulation, 117n.8, 118n.2, 119n.9, 126n.3; open space, 121n.12; planning, 126n.4, 126n.7; pollution, 117n.8; Proposition 1,

Questions for measuring attitudes toward: (*continued*)
123n.3; public problems, 119n.3; public services, 119n.5; road expansions, 124n.10; run-down neighborhoods, 121n.12; Tourist Impact Tax, 126n.5; traffic, 118n.4, 119n.2, 121n.12; water conservation, 117n.8; wildlife, 117n.8

Regional Planning Councils, 27
Resource Planning and Management Committee, findings of, in Keys, 84
Resource shortages, attitudes toward, 95, 97
Road expansions: attitudes toward, 73–80; questions for measuring attitudes toward, 124n.10
Roper Organization, measures of environmental concern, 2–3
Royal Palm Beach, 74
Run-down neighborhoods: fears of, in Delray Beach, 61–62; questions for measuring attitudes toward, 121n.12

St. Johns County, 28
St. Lucie County, 37, 46; elite discourse in, 39
Sanibel Island, 56
Scaling: reasons for popularity of, viii; theory implicit in, viii, 97
Seley, J. E., 122n.1
Shortages, attitudes toward, 97
Social issues, attitudes toward, 16
South Carolina, 21
Structural functionalism, 3–4
Stuart, Florida, 38
Sunrise, Florida, 49–55; attitudes toward land use regulation in, 54–55; attitudes toward services in, 53–54; attitudes toward taxes in, 53; development patterns in, 63; elite discourse in, 63; population growth in, 50; public opinion in, 50–55

Tampa, 28
Taxes: attitudes toward, 53, 69–73; in Delray Beach, 60
Tax revolt: and attenuation theory, 66–67; and population growth, 67
Tourist Impact Tax: assessments of, 87–90; described, 86; effect on issue publics, 92; questions for measuring attitudes toward, 126n.5
Traffic: attitudes toward, 39–41, 50–53, 62, 77–78, 95; questions for measuring attitudes toward, 118n.4, 119n.2, 121n.12
Treasure Coast Region, 37, 54; attitudes toward crime in, 51; counties comprising, 37; elite discourse in, 37–39; growth management policies in, 37–39; population growth in, 37

Uglification: attitudes toward, 95, 97; and environmental concern, 39, 41, 47
Urban development, policies to promote compact, 26–27
Urban growth boundary: in Lee County, 55–56; in Martin County, 38

Vermont, 21
Visibility principle, 95; defined, 64–65

Water conservation: attitudes toward, 30–34; questions for measuring attitudes toward, 117n.8
Water shortages, attitudes toward, 40
West Palm Beach, 74
Wildlife protection: attitudes toward, 30–34, 40, 95; questions for measuring attitudes toward, 117n.8
Wilson, John, 3